100 JOURNEYS FOR THE SPIRIT

CHIEF CONTRIBUTORS
Michael Ondaatje • Joseph Marshall III • Paul Theroux
Andrew Motion • Jan Morris • Mark Tully • Alexander McCall Smith

FOREWORD BY Pico Iyer

Sacred • Inspiring • Mysterious • Enlightening

100 JOURNEYS FOR THE SPIRIT

CHIEF CONTRIBUTORS
Michael Ondaatje • Joseph Marshall III • Paul Theroux
Andrew Motion • Jan Morris • Mark Tully • Alexander McCall Smith

FOREWORD BY Pico Iyer

First published in the United Kingdom and Ireland in 2011 by
Watkins Publishing, an imprint of Duncan Baird Publishers Ltd
Sixth Floor, Castle House
75–76 Wells Street
London W1T 3QH

Conceived, created and designed by Duncan Baird Publishers

Managing Editor: Kirty Topiwala
Editorial Assistant: Elinor Brett
Managing Designer: Manisha Patel
Picture Research: Julia Ruxton

British Library Cataloguing-in-Publication Data:
A CIP record for this book is available from the British Library

ISBN: 978-1-78028-031-8

10 9 8 7 6 5 4 3 2 1

Typeset in Rotis Sans Serif
Colour reproduction by Bright Arts
Printed in Singapore by Imago

NOTES
Abbreviations used throughout this book:
CE Common Era (the equivalent of AD)
BCE Before the Common Era (the equivalent of BC)

contents

foreword

BY PICO IYER

I walked last night into a 12th-century temple set against the eastern hills of Kyoto. It was an illuminated wonderworld: five-pointed maple leaves and camphor trees were lit up by soft lanterns in the warm late-autumn night. Stands of eerily bright bamboo stood over a small waterfall, a teahouse and a small garden. Figures walking in front of the shoji screens of bare tatami rooms looked like silhouettes. Every November, for a few weeks, Shoren-in and other Buddhist temples in the ancient capital of Japan open their gates after nightfall so visitors can enjoy the last flare of colours before the dark of winter.

Yet as I walked among the stone lanterns, along a narrow path beside a pond, my annual autumn pilgrimage, I noticed something even more remarkable. The college kids, grandmothers and other foreigners walking beside me were not at all the people I'd seen waiting on the street outside, 30 minutes before. They, too, were lit up, in less obvious ways, and newly hushed. And the effect was not just because of the cell-phone cameras that flashed to catch them in the same frame as the azaleas. It was as if they had stepped into a kind of natural church, and, whatever their tradition or belief, were ready to let something speak to them. Or even through them.

We all know how we can be turned around by a magic place; that's why we travel, often. And yet we all know, too, that the change cannot be guaranteed. Travel is a fool's paradise, Emerson reminded us, if we think that we can find anything far off that we could not find at home. The person who steps out into the silent emptiness of Easter Island is, alas, too often the same person who got onto the plane the day before at Heathrow, red-faced and in a rage.

Yet still the hope persists and sends us out onto the road: certain places can so shock or humble us that they take us to places inside ourselves, of terror or wonder or the confounding mixture of them both, that we never see amidst the hourly distractions and clutter of home. They slap us awake, and into a recognition of who we might be in our deepest moments. I will never forget walking out onto the terrace of my broken guest-house in Lhasa, in 1985, and seeing the Potala Palace above what was then just a cluster of traditional whitewashed Tibetan houses, its thousand windows seeming to watch over us. I will never forget, too, visiting the Church of the Holy Sepulchre in Jerusalem two years ago and feeling, whether I wanted to or not, all the prayers, hopes and complications that people had brought to it. The place is as dark, irregular and everyday as the fights it houses – as worldly and human as the Potala seems the opposite – and yet the very fact that so many millions have come for centuries to pray and sob among its flickering candles ensures that many more will do so, even if, like me, they're not Christian or Buddhist or anything.

Places have charisma, in short, as much as people do. I've been travelling with the Fourteenth Dalai Lama, from Hiroshima to Zurich to New York to India, for more than 30 years now, and I've noticed how often – almost inevitably – even the most hardened journalists or non-Buddhists break into smiles, or actual tears, when he catches their eye or rubs their hand in his. The same happens with his close friend, the Anglican Desmond Tutu. Charisma (from the Greek, "gifts from the heavens") can't be replicated, and there's no recipe or reason for its existence, but certain places pull us as mysteriously as if they were answering questions we hadn't thought to ask.

So when you encounter the (highly arbitrary) list of special places that fill this book, we hope that you'll be moved to challenge the selection, to add candidates of your own, to ask if Angkor Wat is really more inspiring than Banteay Srei down the road, or whether Bolivia doesn't have a power that Peru might have lost by now. The value of a list like this is to stir you into making up lists of your own, which may include places not so far from home at all. When I was in my mid-twenties I travelled from Bali to Havana to Reykjavik in search of a place that would take me out of time and space. Then, not fully satisfied, I came back, as parable suggests, to my mother's house in California – and found the private heaven I'd been looking for in a monastery three hours' drive up the road.

We travel, as Proust famously said, in search not of new sights, but of new eyes with which to see everything, old sights included. And though those eyes are available to us, as Emerson pointed out, even when we just sit quietly at home, some places so startle or quiet us that we can't help but see things differently. At the end of the last century, an editor at an online magazine asked me to write an essay on a "Sacred Space". He was expecting a piece on Machu Picchu or Stonehenge, I knew, but I wrote about my little blond-wood desk. He asked for a second essay, and I wrote on memory, everything inside me. Yet if I hadn't been to Greece and Burma, if I hadn't stood, wordless, before Ayers Rock and Notre-Dame, I'm not sure that I'd have been able to see how much was available to me at my desk or just by closing my eyes and looking back. A journey of the spirit only starts with somewhere wondrous. It continues wherever we are, through the doors that wonder has opened.

Pico Iyer

Utah, USA

BRYCE CANYON

Where the rocky pillars in most canyons have pinnacles, in Bryce Canyon they are "hoodoos", a name given to them by the Paiute Indians, who inhabited this part of Utah long before Europeans arrived. The Paiute believed that these intricate structures were petrified ancients – part human, part bird, part animal – who were punished for their now unknown crimes by being sentenced to an eternity set in stone. Today the hoodoos form a starkly dramatic feature of a landscape that sometimes seems enchanted, sometimes cursed.

Many evocatively named rock formations decorate the canyon, including the famous Thor's Hammer, which rises majestically from the floor of this extraordinary ravine, looking for all the world like an arm holding a thunderous club – one that might fall at any moment. There are also the Wall of Windows, the Chessmen, Tower Bridge, and the Grand Staircase, each one formed by millennia of erosion. As T. C. Bailey, a government surveyor who visited in 1876, observed with undisguised wonder, "There are deep caverns and rooms resembling ruins of prisons, castles, churches, with their guarded walls, battlements, spires and steeples, niches and recesses, presenting the wildest and the most wonderful scene that the eye of man ever beheld."

These structures are made glorious by the spectrum of at least 60 shades in the limestone, sandstone and mudstone from which they are formed. In the heat of the day, these rich hues seem to hum with vivid warmth; in the evenings they soften and deepen, as the shadows created by every recession and protrusion lengthen. Owing to the lack of artificial light for miles around, when night finally falls the area is plunged into total blackness – a rare experience in the USA these days. Visitors sometimes come for a nighttime viewing, to stare in awe at the 7,500 stars to be seen overhead in a moonless sky.

LEFT: Sunset over the multi-faceted "hoodoos" of Bryce Canyon – structures thought to be petrified ancients by the Paiute Indians.

BELOW: The 28 radiating spokes of the Bighorn Medicine Wheel, believed to be a sacred seasonal clock.

Wyoming, USA

BIGHORN MEDICINE WHEEL

To arrive at the Bighorn Medicine Wheel, at the end of a rough track on a high ridge that lies under snow for nearly ten months a year, is to gain more than just a breathtaking vista of the surrounding Bighorn Mountains of Wyoming. For this enigmatic, centuries-old monument lies at the heart of one of the largest sacred landscapes in the world. At 9,640 feet (3,000 metres) above sea level, the Bighorn Wheel is the most famous and remarkable of up to 150 interrelated sacred sites scattered across a vast swathe of Wyoming, South Dakota, Montana, Alberta and Saskatchewan.

The Wheel is formed from the whitish stones and boulders – glacial debris – that litter the ground in these parts. The stones are laid out in a rough circle almost 100 feet (30 metres) across, with 28 lines of stones radiating from a central "hub" cairn like the spokes of a wheel. Or, more significantly, like the 28 rafters of a Native American ceremonial lodge.

There are five further cairns around the rim, and a sixth just outside it. The outer cairns are actually human being-sized recesses, and a person sitting or crouching in the sixth cairn just before dawn on the summer solstice will see the sun rising exactly behind the central cairn, which perhaps once supported a pole. Another aligns with the solstice sunset, and the cairns also furnish alignments with the heliacal risings (when a star first becomes visible, just before dawn, after the sun has hidden it for a whole season) of the stars Fomelhaut, Aldebaran, Rigel and Sirius.

The Wheel seems, therefore, to have been a kind of sacred seasonal clock, built by one of the Native American peoples of the region, such as the Crow, Cheyenne or Arapaho. Otherwise its purpose is unknown, as are the rites and ceremonies that were once held here in the distant past, infusing it with sacred mystery. As the numerous offerings left at the monument attest, it remains a sacred site for Native Americans and others today, and a powerful locus of "medicine", or spirit power.

Nazca Desert, Peru

NAZCA LINES

Pilots flying the length of Peru's coastal desert know the lands between the Andes and the Pacific Ocean to be among the most desolate on Earth. Occasionally the arid expanse of sand and gravel is broken by the greenery of a river valley, carrying runoff from the high peaks down to the seashore. But in one particular stretch between the Nazca and Ingenio rivers, an unexpected sight breaks the monotony. Hundreds of gigantic markings striate the barren landscape, sketching a phantasmagoria of complex designs. These are the Nazca Lines, and they have lain undisturbed for over a thousand years, barely touched by the eroding power of rain. Understanding of their full scope had to await the development of aviation in the 20th century, for many of the larger designs could only be appreciated from above, looking down from the sky.

The lines first attracted widespread attention through the writings of Eric von Däniken, a controversial Swiss author who claimed that the largest of them, up to 7.5 miles (12 km) long, were designed as landing strips for extraterrestrial spacecraft. Few scholars have taken his theories seriously, but most are happy to admit that there are real mysteries surrounding the figures, which include representational images of dolphins, hummingbirds and other natural phenomena as well as abstract patterns. By all accounts the lines were easy enough to create. All that was required was the removal of a top layer of weathered gravel to reveal the lighter soil underneath. Excavated pebbles were then piled along the sides of the lines to emphasize their silhouettes.

What remains unclear is their purpose. The Nazca culture was at its peak in the 4th and 5th centuries CE. The people who inhabited the river valley at that time created fine pottery, buried their dead in a squatting posture and are known to have practised trepanning. Yet their greatest legacy remains the 350 or so designs they drew in the desert lands to the north, seemingly intended only for the eyes of gods gazing down on this giant open-air gallery from the heavens.

ABOVE: An aerial view of some of the vast, mysterious markings created thousands of years ago in the Peruvian desert by the Nazca people. The top level of gravel was removed to make the marks, which were then outlined with piled-up pebbles.

Panajachel, Guatemala

LAKE ATITLÁN

This highland crater lake has three dramatic volcanoes towering above its southern shore. At dawn, the surface of the lake is silver-grey and calm – empty apart from a few small fishing boats, hollowed from avocado trunks. As the sun heats up, clouds form, obscuring the peaks. By evening, if there's a south wind, there may be 4-foot waves, and the volcanoes become inky silhouettes in the gloaming.

Atitlán, "the place of the water", is the deepest lake in Central America – nobody knows quite how deep. Atitlán holds many mysteries: beneath its surface lie the remains of ancient cities, lost for 2,600 years. Western travellers were drawn to the mystic beauty of Lake Atitlán in the 1960s, and despite three decades of civil war, grey-haired hippy settlers can still be seen in the town on its shore, Panajachel – nicknamed Gringotenango ("place of the gringo"). But in lakeside villages beyond, the indigenous culture is undisturbed. In the village of Santiago Atitlán, devotees worship Maximón, a 3-foot-high wooden figure, whose head is carved anew each year. In these remote highlands, the Maya still wear traditional handwoven clothes, embroidered with flowers and birds, but Maximón wears leather shoes and is draped in dozens of silk scarves. This deity lives as the guest of a local family, moving to a different house each Easter. The hosts decorate a room with bunting, plastic flowers, statues of Jesus and offerings of fruit and vegetables. Rotas of reliable married male relations guard the god, and put him to bed each night.

Each village around the lake has both a Mayan name and a saint's name. Church façades, sturdily built to resist earthquakes and volcanic eruptions, are carved with sacred maize cobs and convolvulus seeds. Inside, painted statues are dressed in local clothes, and shamans perform rituals with smoking herbs. The Maya of Lake Atitlán have successfully adapted the conquistadors' Catholicism and the missionaries' Protestantism to fit their traditional indigenous beliefs.

RIGHT: A jetty overlooking one of the three volcanoes that line Lake Atitlán's southern shore.

ABOVE: The "White House" ruins are the remains of an Anasazi settlement located in a crevasse in the canyon wall. The cliff is more than twice the height of the area captured in this photograph.

RIGHT: Spider Rock marks the junction between Canyon de Chelly and Monument Canyon. The local Navajo people believe that the goddess Spider Woman lives in its tip.

Arizona, USA

CANYON DE CHELLY

This vast and sinuous canyon lies in the heart of Navajo country, between the tribe's four sacred mountains. Cut through the sandstone landscape by a river flowing down from the Tunicha Mountains, the canyon's steep red walls bear the marks, rugged forms and crevices of thousands of years of weathering and erosion: dramatic structural expressions of the passing of time.

Carved into these sheer cliffs, high above the canyon floor in horizontal crevasses, are the ancient dwellings of the prehistoric Native Americans known as the Anasazi (or Ancient Pueblo Peoples). The "White House" settlement, named for its white gypsum backdrop, was built in the 11th century and once housed a community of more than 100 people. Nearby, complex pictographs adorn the walls, with decorative patterns and spirals or narrations of historical events such as the arrival of the Spanish army in the area. Today the region is owned and inhabited by the Navajo people who have occupied it since the 18th century, and the Canyon itself is classed as a national monument.

At the junction between Canyon de Chelly and another canyon, Monument, a great sandstone spear known as Spider Rock rises some 800 feet (240 metres) from the canyon floor, casting a dramatic shadow across the surrounding landscape. In Navajo and Hopi legends the tip of the rock is said to be the home of the goddess Spider Woman – a powerful intermediary between humans and the gods. The Spider Woman is credited with having taught the Navajo weaving, one of their most important crafts. While she is venerated as a protector of her people, she is also feared, and is rumoured to have taken misbehaving children up to her lair to devour them. The towering sacred pinnacle is an important reminder of her presence to the local people.

California, USA

BIG SUR

BY PICO IYER

A stretch of otherworldly coastline

Very often the entire majestic strip of rocky coastline along the Pacific Ocean is cut off from the world for days by fog. All you can hear is the sea pounding against rocks far below. This makes a perfect, poetic sense: more than anywhere I know, the 90-mile stretch of central Californian coastline known as Big Sur, running from San Simeon in the south to Carmel in the north, is a world apart. Its sovereign elements are rocky cliff and redwood forest and unending ocean. Thoughts of the daily world fall miraculously away as soon as you arrive here. It feels, as I've never felt elsewhere in a lifetime of travelling, as if you've entered a different realm in which time and space extend forever.

Big Sur is officially a little lane of shops, along a two-lane road, and barely 2,000 souls scattered across 250 square miles (650 square km) of wilderness. It received its name from Spanish explorers who passed through almost half a millennium ago, daunted by *el país grande del sur*, or "the big country of the south". Until their arrival, the only people who knew this mist-enshrouded world were Esselen and Salinan tribes, living off shellfish and acorns from coastal live oaks. To this day, mudslides after winter rains send whole slopes slipping down, to block off the only connecting road, Highway One, for weeks on end. Forest fires regularly reduce the hills to charred black earth again.

For decades, therefore, those who want to live at a distance from the workaday world – artists and outlaws and renegade mystics – have flocked here, creating a curious, self-sufficient community. The poet Robinson Jeffers built a tower to write in near Carmel, overlooking a region he called "the noblest thing I have ever seen". Henry Miller came to Big Sur from Greece and imagined an ideal community springing up, "God-filled ... even if none of its members believe in God." Jack Kerouac wrote a 22-page poem simply transcribing the surge and crash and sigh of the sea, more than 1,000 feet below. Hunter S. Thompson used to guard the hot-springs baths at the Esalen Institute, which has for nearly half a century brought together explorers of consciousness from Aldous Huxley to Joseph Campbell.

It's perfect that Big Sur is the cradle of the "human potential" movement. When you stay in Deetjen's Big Sur Inn, amidst redwoods older than Christianity (no locks on your door, no telephones or TVs in your wood-stove room), when you sit in Nepenthe restaurant, named after Homer's potion of forgetfulness (nothing visible out to sea but grey whales), you can easily believe that anything is possible. I've been staying on and off for eighteen years in a Catholic hermitage in Big Sur, tucked into the hills above the ocean. At dawn I wake up to bells, and a great bowl of blue sky above, red-tailed hawks above the golden pampas grass and the great, still blue plate of the Pacific far below. Night falls, and all I can see are occasional lights of cars disappearing round the coastline to the south, and more stars than I could dream of counting. Many places offer you beauty, grandeur, spaciousness; none but Big Sur, in my experience, tells you so powerfully that all those blessings lie within.

LEFT, ABOVE: Sand Dollar Beach, one of the many beaches dotted along Big Sur. Visitors often take a break here when driving down the famous Highway One.

LEFT, BELOW: Waves hitting the rocky shore, a familiar sight and sound in Big Sur.

LEFT: Coast redwoods, members of the genus *Sequoia*, to which some of the tallest trees on the planet belong, grow all along the Big Sur coastline. These coastal forests are one of the three "sovereign elements" of Big Sur – the others being rocky cliff and unending sea.

FAR LEFT: Big Sur headlands partially obscured by the fog that regularly enshrouds this area in the summer months.

ABOVE: Stone heads carved into the wall surrounding *Kalasasaya*, or "the temple of stopped stones".

RIGHT: A portal framing a statue of the Tiwanakan deity, the Staff-Bearing God.

near La Paz, Bolivia

TIWANAKU

Some 12,400 feet (3,800 metres) up on the Bolivian altiplano stand some of South America's most evocative ruins. They are all that remain of the city of Tiwanaku, once the capital of a kingdom whose influence stretched from the Pacific coast to northern Argentina. The people who built the city were predecessors of the Inca, and taught the later empire-builders many of their skills in monumental construction.

At its peak in the 7th and 8th centuries CE, the city was not just an administrative hub but also a religious centre, attracting pilgrims from far afield. They came to visit its temples, laid out in a sequence of raised platforms and sunken courts. Today the ruins serve as reminders of the devoted worshippers who gathered here, and the ceremonies that once took place in these structures. The city's chief surviving monument, the Gateway of the Sun, gave onto the central plaza of one of these temples, the Kalasasaya. Carved from a single block of stone, the portal bears an image of the Tiwanakan supreme being, a figure known as the Staff-Bearing God from the staves he clutches in each hand.

The people who built Tiwanaku left few other records, for they had no writing. They managed to wrest a living from the harsh terrain of the treeless puna largely thanks to the proximity of Lake Titicaca. South America's second largest body of fresh water, the lake now lies 12 miles (20 km) to the north but in earlier times lapped the city's fringes. The inhabitants used irrigation to reclaim agricultural land and reared herds of llama and alpacas, which provided meat and wool as well as serving as beasts of burden.

What they left for later generations, however, was their extraordinary architectural prowess. The ceremonial complexes they constructed featured monolithic stone blocks as much as 23 feet long and 13 feet wide (7 metres by 4 metres) and weighing up to 100 tonnes. The fruits of their labours still inspire awe, stimulating local legends of a lost race of giants whose colossal handiwork still adorns the wind-whipped high plains.

Ohio, USA

SERPENT MOUND

Surrounded by steep wooded slopes and a sheer rockface, a prominent, curving ridge snakes above Ohio Brush and East Creeks in Adams County, Ohio. "Snakes" is the right word, for around a thousand years ago, ca. 1050CE, the local Fort Ancient people chose this tapering ridge as the place to construct one of the world's largest and most remarkable earthworks – a long, sinuous mound, 20 feet (6 metres) wide and around 3 feet (1 metre) high, in the form of a great serpent, an effigy so big that it can be seen in its entirety only from the sky.

Beginning at the western end of the ridge, the perfect counterclockwise spiral of the serpent's coiled tail unwinds along the top of the ridge in gentle undulations for another 1,150 feet (350 metres) or so. Finally, the serpent's head appears, the jaws of the snake appearing to hold an enormous egg, an oval enclosure at the eastern tip of the ridge.

Why was this built? What rites took place here? Snakes are important in many Native American cultures as symbols of fertility and regeneration. The idea of a "cosmic serpent" or "cosmic egg" as the source of existence is also found elsewhere in the world. The head of the Serpent Mound points to the sunset on the summer solstice, and undulations of its body may also point to other events, such as the equinox and winter solstice sunrises. Was the "egg" in fact the sun, "swallowed" by the cosmic serpent at midsummer, the turning point of the year? The body has seven undulations, a number with significance in Native American lore, as when Native peoples acknowledge their responsibility to those who will come after, down to "the seventh generation".

Perhaps the Serpent Mound was the dramatic setting of a regular sacred renewal rite that acknowledged the start of the sun's journey toward winter, and encouraged its return. Although these questions can never be answered for certain, the site retains its mystery and power.

RIGHT: The magnificent winding body of the Serpent Mound. This unexplained effigy is more than 1,250 feet (380 metres) long.

BELOW: The present-day Basilica of Sainte-Anne-de-Beaupré, rebuilt in 1926 after a fire. The basilica is associated with healing miracles and is an important Catholic pilgrimage site.

Quebec, Canada

BASILICA OF SAINTE-ANNE-DE-BEAUPRÉ

That the Basilica of Sainte-Anne-de-Beaupré exists today is a testament to the endurance of a group of French pioneers and missionaries who struggled to establish a community along the banks of the St Lawrence river in Quebec in 1650. In snowshoes and canoes the settlers searched for a site on which to build their village. "New France" was a hostile environment, but the harsh weather and constant danger of attack from the Iroquois Indians were tempered by the fertile soil of the Beaupré hillside ... and, gradually, a small community began to flourish.

With them, on their voyage across the Atlantic, the pioneers brought a devotion to a lesser-known saint, the mother of the Virgin Mary, Anne. The holy grandmother was the patron saint of sailors and the pioneers raised a little wooden church in her name. In 1658, as the first foundation stones were laid, St Anne performed her first miraculous act for the town of Beaupré. A carpenter by the name of Louis Grimond, severely afflicted with rheumatism, laid the first three stones of the church and was instantly healed.

Over the years, the church became a place of pilgrimage for French Canadians and Native Americans alike. It was enlarged repeatedly until a basilica was built in 1876. The structure has been demolished again and again by fires, storms and renovations, the most recent being a terrible fire in 1922, when the basilica was all but destroyed. But each time it has been rebuilt, grander and more glorious than before.

Today, the basilica stands within spacious gardens, its walls resplendent white against the blue northern sky. Inside, 240 stained-glass windows flood the space with softly suffused light, while the simply carved wooden pews remember the structure's humble origins. A statue of St Anne holding the infant Mary is carved from a single piece of oak, and wears a golden crown set with jewels. Stacks of walking sticks, crutches and folded wheelchairs, discarded by the healed, pay homage to the miraculous power of faith that has characterized visitors to Sainte-Anne-de-Beaupré for more than 350 years.

CHRIST THE REDEEMER STATUE

The statue of Christ the Redeemer bestrides a 2,300-foot (700-metre) mountain named Corcovado ("Hunchback"), weighing 635 tons, standing 130 feet (40 metres) tall, and measuring 98 feet (30 metres) from the tip of one outstretched hand to the other. The statistics alone are awe-inspiring.

However, the unique place that Cristo Redentore occupies in the hearts of all Brazilians depends on its sheer visibility. There's barely a sunlit beach or a shadowy *favela* (shanty town) in the entire city from which the colossal, reinforced concrete and soapstone image of the Saviour cannot be seen, his arms held apart in distant benediction.

The sheer scale of the structure means that humans are dwarfed when they stand at its foot – only by leaning back at an impossible angle can they glimpse the carved features of Christ. And of course, while many choose to look upward to contemplate the face of divine power, others direct their gaze downward, over the breathtaking panorama that encompasses both the natural splendours of the surrounding coastline and the rampant urban sprawl that characterizes the restlessness of Rio.

Given the difficulty in accessing the site, up torturous, twisting roads, it's not hard to believe that the statue took nine years to build, between 1922 and 1931. Nor that in a fiercely Catholic country, a small chapel should have been built within its base dedicated to the Marian apparition, *Nossa Senhora Aparecida* ("Our Lady of the Apparition"), patron saint of all Brazil.

Symbol of hope, constant reminder of God's presence, Christ the Redeemer serves not just as the guardian of the people who live in its shadow, but as a constant companion through all their joys and travails. Although it stands thousands of feet above sea level, the statue's foundations are rooted in Brazil's very soul.

ABOVE: The striking figure of the enormous Christ the Redeemer statue can be seen from almost any point in the city of Rio de Janeiro.

Wyoming, USA

DEVILS TOWER

BY JOSEPH MARSHALL III

A monument to lift the spirit

Reaching for the heavens as it rises out of the sage brush, pine trees and sparse prairie grass of northeast Wyoming is a scarred monolith that overwhelms the surrounding landscape. To scientists and tourists this is the core of an ancient volcano. To the many indigenous tribes who lived, and live, on the northern plains of North America, it is a holy place.

Once, in ancient times, seven girls were picking berries when a ferocious bear began to chase them. Fleeing to the top of a small hill, the girls huddled in terror and prayed to the Great Spirit for deliverance. The Great Spirit answered their desperate pleas by raising the hill higher and higher until the girls were safely out of the bear's reach. The enraged beast tried in vain to climb up after them, scratching and clawing with increasing fury at the sides of the hill, which had now become a tall mountain. Eventually, the bear gave up and slunk off, and the Great Spirit carried the girls safely back to their village.

This, according to one Native tradition, is how the vast protrusion of igneous rock known as Devils Tower came into being. Native tribes have known it by many names, including Bear's Lodge, Bear's Lair, Aloft on a Rock, and Ghost Mountain. The bear's long, deep claw marks can still be seen in the form of the strikingly regular columns of igneous rock that give all sides of the mountain its remarkable appearance, like a colossal scratched tree stump – hence another of the Native names, Tree Rock. The official name, Devils Tower, derives from "Bad Spirit Mountain", a 19th-century mistranslation of Bear's Lodge, the most common name of the site among Native tribes.

The mountain – which was declared America's first National Monument in 1906 – has long drawn visitors for its sheer breathtaking beauty. Standing nearly 1,300 feet (400 metres) above the prairie floor, it has near-vertical sides that are a stark challenge to any of the thousands of rock climbers who come here every year to test their skills and fortitude. In June, however, most – but sadly not all – recreational climbers stay away, respecting the desire of Native peoples not to be disturbed in traditional sacred rituals and ceremonies at the foot of the mountain, such as the sun dance, sweat lodge rites, vision quests and prayer offerings. For untold generations, and long before any human climber thought to scale its heights, different tribes have performed rites at the base in order to honour the Great Spirit and reaffirm their ancient attachment to the mountain.

Whether in groups or as individual pilgrims, many Native people still go to Devils Tower to pray, seek guidance, meditate, and connect with the Earth and the heavens. In my view, and as the legend of the seven girls vividly acknowledges, Devils Tower has one common effect: it lifts – both literally and figuratively. Whether your journey to the mountain is a recreational or spiritual one, whether it causes you to lift your eyes to its summit, or climb its sheer walls, or offer prayers to be sent upward, it will leave you with the unmistakable sense of having approached closer to a higher realm.

RIGHT: Devils Tower or Bear's Lodge is actually the core of an ancient volcano. The site of vision quests and sacred ceremonies for native tribes, the monolith has many associated legends. One tells how it sprang up to save seven girls from a great bear who was chasing them. The grooves in its sides are said to be the marks left by the bear's claws.

Lighthouse Reef, Belize

THE GREAT BLUE HOLE

From space, this giant underwater sinkhole looks like a great prehistoric eye – a deep indigo-blue pupil with an iris of palest turquoise, delineating the coral reef that surrounds it.

The Great Blue Hole was once a vast Ice Age cave system, riddling the limestone that now makes up the bed of the Lighthouse Reef, off the coast of Belize. As the ice melted and the caves became submerged in water, their roofs collapsed forming a sinkhole of astonishing size. Over 1,000 feet (300 metres) in diameter, the water at the lip of the hole is only a few feet deep at high tide but then plunges to a depth of 410 feet (125 metres), making it a coveted destination for scuba divers, including the conservationist and explorer Jacques Yves Cousteau, who led an expedition here in 1972.

The shallower waters abound with marine life: coral reefs sustain anemones, shrimp and neon-coloured gobies. Angelfish, Butterflyfish, Parrotfish and sea turtles inhabit this aquatic jungle. Plunge further into the chasm, though, and the waters become clearer and almost motionless as the light filters away and marine life becomes scarcer. At a depth of 230 feet (70 metres), the cave is coated with silt, and stalactites hang from monstrous overhangs in the darkness. Intrepid divers, descending to about 135 feet (40 metres), have found the remains of sea turtles, and rare sightings of bull sharks and hammerheads have been reported. Floating here, you experience a sense of total immersion, aware only of the stillness, the vast expanse of water and your breath moving in and out – an act of pure meditation.

ABOVE AND LEFT: The Great Blue Hole reaches astonishing depths, attracting many adventurous scuba divers.

Hawaii, USA

MAUNA KEA VOLCANO

Legend has it that Mauna Kea, or "White Mountain", one of the five great volcanoes that make up the island of Hawaii, is home to the snow goddess Poliahu. Daughter of the sky god Kane, she is as venerated by the farmers whose lands her melting streams water, as Pele, the goddess of fire, who lives on neighbouring volcano Mauna Loa, is feared.

It is said that these two female deities fell out many centuries ago over a holua contest, the traditional Hawaiian sport in which large, wooden sleds race at breakneck speed down grassy hillsides. In a bid to thwart the progress of Poliahu's holua, Pele summoned up rivers of volcanic lava from her home on nearby Mauna Loa, or Long Mountain. In order to stem the molten tide of lava, Poliahu laid in its path the frosty white mantle of snow which sits atop Mauna Kea for most of the year.

Mauna Kea is dormant, and according to scientific calculations it is more than 4,000 years now since it last erupted. Meanwhile, malevolent Mauna Loa still grumbles to this day, its intermittent emissions causing anxious looks from residents of the island's capital, Hilo. They even have

a name for the strands of fibrous volcanic ash that fly through the air: Pele's hair.

As befits a place with such supernatural resonances, Mauna Kea is for many Hawaiians a place of pilgrimage: they walk among its eerie cinder cones, in search of their *mana*, or divine power. Owing to the altitude, the air up here is thin and rarefied: technically, Mauna Kea is the world's tallest mountain, rising 33,000 feet (10,000 metres) from the Pacific seabed, although only 13,700 of these feet (4,200 metres) are above sea level. In the dark of the night, Mauna Kea offers a view of the heavens so clear and breathtaking that it not only bewitches casual stargazers but also attracts scores of professional astronomers who occupy the little white observatories dotted across the mountain's lunar landscape.

BELOW: Cinder cones, the dramatic hills formed from volcanic debris, north of the summit of Mauna Kea.

PYRAMID OF THE MAGICIAN

Known by various names, among them Pyramid of the Soothsayer and Pyramid of the Magician, this great structure is fabled to have appeared overnight, erected by a charmed dwarf to win a life or death wager with a ruthless king. This is a fascinating story, but as evidence of human perseverance the truth is almost more remarkable. Over hundreds of years from the 7th century CE, the citizens of the ancient Mayan city of Uxmal, now in Mexico, built a nested set of five temples to honour their rain god, Chaac, their construction reflecting the complex Mayan vision of cosmology.

The result is an architectural marvel, unlike any other such pyramid thanks to its rounded base, tremendous height – more than 115 feet (35 metres) – and steep angle of ascent. Like the rest of Uxmal, it's also uncommonly well preserved, and a journey to the "House of the Magician", the uppermost of the temples, via the various external staircases is not so different now from what it might have been a thousand years ago.

An image of Chaac's gaping mouth forms the doorway in the temple façade, and masks of his face and lattice work are carved elsewhere. At lower levels, the Maya decorated their pyramids sparsely, but the details become ever more ornate on the way up – giving visitors as they climb the sense that they are leaving the quotidian world behind in favour of a holier sphere. Although the rain gods and the Maya are gone, driven out by Spanish invaders in the 16th century, the ruins of Uxmal and its most renowned temple retain much of their original sense of sanctity.

Elsewhere, the conquering Spanish – perhaps unnerved by a spirituality beyond their understanding – sought to tame other pyramids with names from their own tradition. Here, though, it seems they knew not to try, and have left the magician-dwarf well alone.

Chichén Itza, Mexico

WELL OF SACRIFICE

Nineteenth-century travellers to the ruined Mayan city of Chichén Itza in the north of Mexico's Yucatán Peninsula sensed the sinister aura of the *cenote* or sinkhole that lay within its bounds. Almost 200 feet (60 metres) across, its murky green waters lie at the bottom of a natural bowl of limestone 65 feet (20 metres) deep whose perpendicular sides provide just enough light and space for some greenery to grow in crevices and on ledges. "A mysterious influence seemed to pervade it," one early visitor wrote, "in union with the historical account that [the well] was a place of pilgrimage, and that human victims were thrown into it in sacrifice."

Investigations in the early 20th century were to prove the legends true. The remains of at least 42 individuals were recovered from the *cenote*'s depths, sacrificed in return for promises of a blissful afterlife in the care of the gods. Yet now, more than 500 years after the last victims died in its waters, the well has lost most of its malevolent associations. The terror has gone, and the spot exudes a deep sense of peace.

The *cenote* was a central ceremonial feature of a city that was the chief ornament of the final phase of Mayan civilization, around the 1st millennium CE. Chichén Itza was the capital of the Itza, a people who had links to the Toltec culture of central Mexico hundreds of miles to the northwest. They were successful traders and warriors, and their wealth is today attested by thousands of surviving artefacts elegantly fashioned from copper, jade, obsidian and gold – mostly rescued from the *cenote* waters, where they had been thrown as offerings to the gods.

Alaska, USA

WRANGELL-ST ELIAS NATIONAL PARK

The "Mountain Kingdom" of North America is a spectacular wilderness: vast and rugged. Not only is this the largest national park in the United States (six times the size of Yellowstone), but it encompasses the continent's largest group of glaciers and peaks above 16,000 feet (5,000 metres), including Mount St Elias, the second highest peak in the US.

Wrangell-St Elias forms the junction of four major mountain ranges at the Canadian-Alaskan border: the Wrangells, the St Elias, the Chugach and the Nutzotin. The vast body of wilderness has remained mostly untouched since the days when it was the preserve of the first nations, of the Tlingit and the Chugach. The native peoples lived in harmony with their surroundings, worshipping their gods in cathedrals of rock, spruce and cloud. Their shaman priests, healers and guides could summon the spirits of the earth and of the animals. Their world was one of natural dichotomies still apparent today: earth and air, forest and sea, fire and ice.

Mount Wrangell is an active volcano. Covered in a perpetual blanket of snow, the high country is an ice-land of glacier and gun-metal rock. The Copper River winds its way around the Wrangell range and down toward the sea through forests of conifers, blueberry and prickly rose. Moose and caribou graze; grizzly and black bears roam. The river teems with fish: salmon spawn by the million. The range also holds abundant copper deposits that were mined by settlers in the early 1900s at the Kennecott Mining Co. in the heart of the park.

Kennecott is abandoned now – a ghost town. The mine is in disrepair, its red timbered frame slumping against the hill. Though the human presence has diminished, the 13.2 million acres of parkland still abound in wildlife. Wrangell-St Elias evokes a feeling of complete isolation, and the opportunity to immerse oneself totally in an unexplored country.

RIGHT: A pond formed by water from the Kennecott glacier in Wrangell-St Elias National Park.

Minnesota, USA

PIPESTONE

BY JOSEPH MARSHALL III

A place of peace

Lying in the southwest corner of Minnesota, on the edge of beautiful, wide open, tall grass prairie, Pipestone National Monument is named for the soft reddish stone that is quarried here. But the 50-odd quarries are no commercial venture: this is sacred ground, and Native Americans alone are permitted to take the rare stone, just as their ancestors have done for thousands of years – often after travelling hundreds of miles from their home territories.

Native legend has it that the Great Spirit himself gave the red clay stone to all tribes in order to make sacred pipes. To this day the rare pipestone, or catlinite, is fashioned into pipe bowls that are fitted to long wooden stems and used in sacred ceremonies, their smoke carrying prayers to the ancestors and to the Great Spirit himself. Every summer, despite a waiting list of many years for permission, people from many different Native tribes continue to make the long trip to dig the stone.

As well as these descendants of the first seekers of the red stone, many others also come here to experience the place's quiet beauty. Along the trails around Pipestone Creek time has carved tall outcrops of the rock into remarkable "statues" with names such as Old Stone Face and Two Indian Faces. The most striking is probably the Oracle, with its stern profile of a wise and dignified elder. These stone guardians watch over tranquil woodlands, the gently cascading Winnewissa Falls, and grounds where Native peoples perform the traditional sun dance ceremony. Also nearby are the Three Maidens, glacial boulders deposited here thousands of years ago by the side of Lake Hiawatha, named for the heroine of Henry Wadsworth Longfellow's famous 1855 poem, "The Song of Hiawatha", which mentions the sacred pipestone quarries.

Longfellow actually never went to the quarries, but was inspired by the descriptions of the first documented white visitor, the Pennsylvania artist George Catlin, who travelled extensively on the northern plains and made important visual records of several tribes. Catlin, who reached the site in 1836, saw the quarries and took samples of the soft, easily worked, pinkish to blood-red stone that now bears his name.

For many years the predominant Native presence in the region of the pipestone quarries were the Dakota and Nakota, two thirds of the nation that also includes the Lakota. After many years of encroachment on the area, during which most of the tribes were moved westward onto reservations and the small town of Pipestone grew up a mile south of the sacred quarries, the 282-acre site became Minnesota's first National Monument area in 1937, and tribes could once again quarry here freely and exclusively.

Early white observers mistakenly called the sacred pipes "peace pipes", because the Dakota, Nakota and other Plains tribes used them at formal treaty ceremonies with the whites. In one sense, though, the name is apt, because tradition has it that the Great Spirit declared the pipestone grounds a holy place where weapons were banned and where warring tribes must quarry peacefully side by side. Although the hostilities between tribes are mostly in the past, their descendants have not forgotten that their ancestors once put aside their weapons and their troubles when they set foot on the site. Entering Pipestone today, Native peoples make a profound connection with their ancient spiritual traditions. For others, the beauty of the site alone is likely to bring a sense of inner calm. The site remains, for all who come here, a place of peace.

RIGHT: Shadows falling on the pink stone that gives Pipestone its name. Sacred to Native Americans, the stone has been quarried for thousands of years to make pipe bowls for use in sacred ceremonies.

Provence, France

SÉNANQUE ABBEY

In summer the air around Sénanque Abbey is filled with the scent of flowering lavender and the sound of Gregorian chanting which reverberates from within its grey stone walls. This is one of three important Cistercian monasteries in Provence, known collectively as the "three sisters". Located in a secluded valley, its architecture has a pared down simplicity and harmony of elements that suggests tranquillity, permanence and contemplation.

Cistercian monks came here in 1148, from Mazan Abbey in the Ardèche. The impoverished monks lived in huts until they obtained the patronage of the seigneurs of Simiane, enabling them to found the abbey church in 1178. The Cistercians were a particularly ascetic branch of Catholicism founded in 1098 and spread during the 12th century largely thanks to the work of Bernard of Clairvaux. Unlike other monks, Cistercians did not depend on tithes or tolls for their income but worked the land instead. Sénanque monks still grow lavender and tend honey bees for their livelihood.

Cistercian monastic life has an emphasis upon discipline, humility and austerity, and Cistercian architecture typically reflects this. Sénanque's design is based on the Cistercian mother house, Cîteaux Abbey near Dijon, although because of the narrow space of the valley, Sénanque's liturgical east faces north. Conditions are simple, the only heated room being the calefactory where the monks read and write, and there is scarcely any ornament. There are no stained-glass windows, paintings or illuminated manuscripts and the paired limestone columns of the cloisters have only the simplest leaf and vine carvings at their capitals. Decoration is provided instead by the intense mauve of the surrounding lavender fields, the play of light and shade on the abbey walls and the stark black and white habits of passing resident monks.

LEFT: Lavender growing in front of Sénanque Abbey. The abbey's architecture reflects the simplicity and austerity of Cistercian monastic life.

Uffington, England

THE WHITE HORSE

As beautiful as it is mysterious – a stylized chalk figure of a white horse in full flight, hewn out of the turf of the Berkshire Downs thousands of years ago. But for what purpose?

Some claim this is a tribute to the Celtic horse goddess Epona. Some say it commemorates the victory of the Saxon king Alfred over the Danes, in 861CE. Others maintain that the creature is not a horse, but rather the dragon that was slain by St George on nearby Dragon Hill, which has on its summit a bare chalk patch, where the dragon's blood was spilled, and on which (it is said) no grass will ever grow.

Archaeologists have concluded that the White Horse is at least 3,000 years old. Its earliest written reference comes in a monastic manuscript dated between 1074 and 1082, referring to a *mons albi equi* – "hill of the white horse".

About the only thing that can be established for certain is that the horse was created by digging 3-foot-deep trenches, into which crushed chalk fragments were then poured. In medieval times, a ritual "scouring" festival was held every seven years, at which encroaching grass would be trimmed back, and fresh chalk added to maintain the crisp elegance of the tapering lines.

The greatest puzzle of all is how the makers of the White Horse managed to create a figure that can only be appreciated in its entirety from several thousand feet in the air (the beast is 110 feet/34 metres tall and 374 feet/114 metres long). This, more than anything, lends weight to the theory that the White Horse was intended for divine rather than mortal eyes.

Finnmark, Norway

ALTA FJORD ROCK CARVINGS

Humanity can be defined by a common desire for communication, the need to tell a story, or to leave marks – something especially evident at certain sites around the Norwegian town of Alta, where mysterious ancient carvings have been etched into the rocks.

In their natural state these petroglyphs are invisible to the naked eye until water is trickled over them. Then, angular shapes become visible – figures building boats, fishing or playing musical instruments appear alongside herds of reindeer and sacred bear-gods. When a new carving is discovered, red ochre paint is poured into the grooves to make the lines clear. Thousands of years ago, when the designs were fresh, they were probably decorated in a similar way.

The people who made these carvings remain shrouded in mystery. The 5,000 odd etchings date from between ca. 4200 and 500 BCE. Most of them are at a place known as Jiepmaluokta, which means "Bay of Seals" in the local Sami dialect, and are nearly all that remains of a prehistoric settlement. Many of the people and animals in the petroglyphs have tracks trailing behind them, to suggest the direction of their movement. Most seem to move in parallel with the ground, on a horizontal plane. However, bears, animals venerated by many of the ancient tribes of northern Europe, are sometimes depicted as moving vertically upward, across the tracks of the other animals, a detail which has been interpreted as connecting them to the afterlife.

A network of boardwalks allows people to move over the carvings, following them from the highest, earliest petroglyphs, down to the more recent marks, which creep closer to the beach below. To stare at these boldly rendered images, bright red against grey stone, and try to decipher their message, is to experience a profound connection with another people, a connection that transcends time and our ignorance of the facts.

Torcello, Venice

CATHEDRAL OF SANTA MARIA ASSUNTA

BY JAN MORRIS

Island sanctuary of holy, melancholy wonder

Spirituality fights a bitter battle in the city of Venice, invested as the Serenissima is by all the worldly influences of profit and publicity, but it still infuses the watery wasteland of the Venetian Lagoon, the 200-odd square miles of shallow tidal water that is the true hinterland of the place. Small islands are scattered across this water world, boats and barges swarm about it, cruise liners plough through it, but still it possesses something of the transcendent, the feeling that it is, so to speak, fundamentally more than itself.

Even today it can be very lonely in the far reaches of the lagoon, where only barnacled poles guide the navigator among the mud banks, and the tower-crowned silhouette of the city seems hardly more than a hallucination. But out there transcendental treasures survive, and for my money the most marvellous of them all is on the little island of Torcello, whose solitary *campanile* stands like a sentinel eight or nine miles from the city.

Torcello is at least as old as Venice itself. When scavengers out of the pagan North put paid to the Pax Romana in this part of Italy, refugees fled for safety into the uncharted lagoon, and a group from the coastal town of Altinum, led by their bishop, settled on the island of Torcello to start a new city of their own. It never matched the magnificence of Venice itself, similarly founded on a group of larger islands, but in its medieval heyday it was a place of great consequence, with its own ships, industries and mercantile connections. In the 1500s, we are told, some 20,000 people lived there. But Torcello fell into decay as Venice rose to glory. Its streets and palaces crumbled, its harbour was silted up, its inhabitants deserted it, and by Victorian times the island seemed to

ABOVE: An aerial view of the island of Torcello and the surrounding lagoon, the *campanile* (bell tower) of the Cathedral of Santa Maria Assunta clearly visible.

LEFT: The cathedral at sunset, viewed from across the waters of the lagoon. The snow-covered Alps of the mainland can just be glimpsed in the background.

visitors a very emblem of melancholy, an object-lesson in the transience of pride – a lesser example, in fact, of the destiny that had humiliated Venice itself.

Torcello is still a popular tourist destination – just the place for a quick trip from the city, an al fresco lunch and a look at the local sights; but when in the afternoon the tourists leave again, with a last rumble of engines and snapping of cameras, a celestial peace falls upon the island. Only a handful of people live here nowadays, the old sense of allegorical regret is still potent, and nowhere in the world could be much calmer. Then is the time to enter the holy wonder of the place, the cathedral church of Santa Maria Assunta.

From the outside this building looks stern, stark and defensive, rather fortress-like, its immense red-brick *campanile* towering above the island, its windows protected by enormous stone shutters against storms and warfare. Inside, though, its spell is gentle. And this is because almost the very first thing you see, as you enter the high marbled authority of the nave, is the mosaic of the Teotoca Madonna, the God-Bearer, to my mind one of the supreme glories of spiritual art. She stands tall, slender and regretful in the rounded apse above the high altar, and there are tears on her cheeks. I once heard a child describe her as "a tall young lady, holding God".

She is a commanding figure, but commanding only in the gentlest sort of way – commanding us to be kind, commanding us to marvel at the meaning of the baby in her arms, commanding us to realise that the world need not all be power and wealth in a metropolis, but can be just as fulfilled in an old empty church on a lonely island. She is reminding us with her tears, though, that sadness must always be part of life's beauty, and she is surely urging us towards tolerance. More than a thousand years ago Torcello was born out of enmities, conflicts racial, ideological, theological and yes, even spiritual. Clashing cultures sent the refugees to this island, and the Teotoca with them, and God knows they are not all reconciled even now.

ABOVE: A 12th-century mosaic in the apse above the high altar depicting the enormous, elongated figure of the Teotoca Madonna, with the apostles assembled below.

RIGHT: The cathedral nave was rebuilt in the 11th century, the marble Corinthian columns appropriated from classical Greek buildings. The intricate floor patterns are composed of sanded stone and glass.

Mývatn, Iceland

GOÐAFOSS WATERFALL

With frequent rain, winter snows and melting glaciers, Iceland is a land of many waterfalls. Although not the highest – the drop is about 40 feet (12 metres) – Goðafoss is one of the most powerful and dramatic. The river Skjálfandafljót divides here, thundering each side of the island of Hrútey, falling in two deafening horseshoe arcs into a wild, swirling pool below. White spray hovers in the air, far above the falls, blurring the panorama beyond. The waterfall has a primeval power, with its ear-splitting noise, unimaginable volume of water, dangerous churning currents, and unstoppable force. Only 60 miles (100 km) from the Arctic Circle, Goðafoss is also a place of midnight summer sun and, in winter, absolute darkness.

However, the falls are not timeless. Geologically speaking, they are recent and mutable. This volcanic region of north-east Iceland marks the dividing line between the European and North American tectonic plates. Here is the process of continental drift in action, with steam jets, sulphur slopes, boiling mud pits, smoking craters, hot lagoons, lava pillars, and arid highland desert, black and eerie.

The falls have a religious significance, recorded as early as the 11th century by Ari the Wise. Iceland was first settled in the 9th century by pagan Viking Norsemen. When King Olaf of Norway converted to Christianity in 1000CE, he forced all Vikings to adopt his faith but the Icelanders refused. King Olaf cut off trade, and civil war looked likely. Lawspeaker Thorgeir, a pagan priest, was appointed arbitrator, and after 24 hours' contemplation, lying under a fur blanket, he decided that the island should become Christian but that pagan rituals such as eating horseflesh and killing surplus children could continue in private. To demonstrate his commitment to Christianity, Thorgeir threw all his pagan idols into the waterfall, and it has been known as Goðafoss – God's Falls – ever since.

RIGHT: The thundering Goðafoss falls, divided in two by the island of Hrútey.

Amsterdam, Netherlands

OUDE KERK

The Oude Kerk is so named because it is the oldest church in Amsterdam, consecrated in 1306. Rising up from the heart of what is now the city's red light district, it gives the impression of having grown organically out of the surrounding buildings and streets. The Oude Kerk is truly a church of the people, a cohesion of the sacred and the profane.

The building is huge, covering 35,520 square feet (3,300 square metres), and is the product of continual renovations and alterations. Over the past 700 years, the Oude Kerk has metamorphosed as frequently and naturally as the city itself, and now contains almost as many chapels as there have been phases of building. Its floor is paved with 2,500 gravestones belonging to its congregation, and some 10,000 citizens of Amsterdam are buried under its foundations.

The church was once known as the "common room of the city". In the early 16th century, before the puritanical purges of the Calvinists, the building was filled with the comings and goings of the local people. Oude Kerk was the shelter of vagrants and tramps, the market place for pedlars, and the social hub for assignations of all kinds. After 1566, however, the homeless were banned from the church and the building was cleaned out, stripped of its images of saints and its altars, its wall paintings covered over with whitewash.

Today, the Oude Kerk has become a destination for tourists and pilgrims alike. Walking through the vast, cool spaces, the visitor is bombarded with countless echoes from the past, and with the music of its two magnificent organs. Its medieval oak vault, the largest of its kind in Europe, boasts impeccable acoustics and several prominent orchestras and choirs still use the church for recordings. Despite the best efforts of the Calvinists, Oude Kerk retains the indelible mark of the souls who have shaped it and who rest inside its walls.

LEFT: The vast nave of the Oude Kerk, Amsterdam's oldest church. The interior has been pale and sparsely decorated since the Calvinist purges of the 16th century.

Brittany, France
CARNAC

Stand in the fields next to the hamlet of Le Ménec, on the outskirts of Carnac, as the sun breaks through the sea mists that often roll in off the Gulf of Morbihan. A line of eleven great stones emerge from the mist, towering over the visitor in the dawn light. As the mist lifts, more stones appear, ranked behind the leaders like a column of soldiers, and stretching off into the distance for almost a mile.

The Carnac alignments lie at the heart of a Neolithic sacred landscape that encompasses around 100 large and small alignments, enclosures, barrows and single standing stones. Research suggests an origin as far back as ca. 5000BCE – which would mean that, astonishingly, the megaliths were shaped, transported and erected by people who knew nothing of the wheel and had tools of only bone and stone.

Why were they erected? Breton legend saw them as a column of Roman troops – petrified while pursuing a Christian saint – and ascribed fertility properties to them. Early antiquarians linked them with the Druids. Their orientation suggests a connection with the summer and winter solstices. Large stone enclosures mark the ends of the alignments, and it is natural to assume that they served a ritual function.

It also appears that the alignments were not erected all at once: generation after generation added stones, perhaps in homage to ancestors or as an act of commemoration. The stones decrease in size from west to east, so that looking westward down the rows, they all look roughly the same size. Mysterious and magnificent, these megaliths continue to dominate all later human imprints on the landscape.

Orkney, Scotland

THE RING OF BRODGAR

The Ring of Brodgar is one of the finest of stone circles, and one of the most beautifully sited. At 340 feet (105 metres), the circle is exhilaratingly wide, giving the visitor a sense of order lightly applied to a majestic age-old landscape – lightly but strongly, for it has stood more than 4,000 years. Twenty-seven monoliths survive, of heights up to 13 feet (4 metres): it's thought there were 60 originally. Wandering around you experience a sense of inexpressible, earth-rooted beauty.

Loosely speaking, this is a "henge" – the word has an air of antiquarian mystery. On one stone on the northern side there's a Norse runic inscription: the Vikings often came this way, leaving graffiti in sacred spots. The monument stands on the Ness of Brodgar, a thin cape separating two sea lochs, and this word also leads us to the Vikings, for it comes from *nes* ("nose") in Old Norse. Nearby is an isolated menhir, or large standing stone, the Comet Stone. The stones

themselves are surrounded by a rock-cut ditch, with two entrance causeways.

It seems likely that sight lines connecting individual stones with notches in the surrounding hills pointed to sunrises or sunsets on significant days of the year. Various outlying menhirs might also be part of the pattern of alignments. The stones were quarried from different sites on Orkney, and in the building there may have been an element of collective enterprise, binding communities together; or, conversely, of competition. Perhaps the sacred enclosure was used for a variety of purposes. Today the best approach is simply to offer oneself up to the wonder of it all, especially on a long summer day of fickle weather. To gaze on a rainbow over the Ring brings you close to transcendence. Fleeting God-given colour and enduring worshipful stone offer as great a contrast as you could ever find on this Earth.

Essex, England

ST PETER-ON-THE-WALL

BY ANDREW MOTION

Church of ancient simplicity, alive with the whispers of the past

We think of the Home Counties as tamed, but each has its pockets of wildness. Essex certainly does. Perched on a remote part of its sea-fringe is one of the most beautifully simple and ancient churches in England. I first came here as a child; my mother thought I should see it. "A church, mum?" I was incredulous. "Yes, but a very old one." We toiled through dormitory towns and drowsy villages, then straightened onto the bump of land between the Blackwater and the Crouch. The earth crumbled into black sand. A power station threatened the horizon, then sank from sight. And there was ... the church, obviously, but hardly a church at all. More like a stone barn. A tall, narrow stack of stones, with a steeply pitched roof, a plain wooden door beneath a little domed window, and walls mended haphazardly with farmer's rubble.

The building is probably the nave of the original church founded by St Cedd in the early 650s, similar in design to the earliest Saxon churches. This makes it one of the earliest surviving churches in England. (Round about, preserving their riddles under the windswept grass, are the remains of the chancel and side chambers.) The materials are Roman – brick, ashlar and septaria, much of it taken from the fort that once stood nearby, long since levelled. I learned all this on later visits. But these visits were more than just returns. They were little pilgrimages, homecomings in the years after my mother's death, when I could stare though the wrong end of time's telescope and see us in miniature, arriving together for the first time, sitting down and whispering in the always-empty space. So many centuries of prayer; such a store of questioning.

Everything inside the church is a miracle of survival. But there's the outside as well, and the way it mixes with the inside, so the church feels dwarfed and affirmed by the place it occupies. By the salt wind streaming over the ruins of the fort and turning the grass into a lake of mercury. By the enormous sky, gilded by Channel-light as it brews its cloud-concoctions, flatters them with shafts of sun, then dismantles them as though none of their beauty mattered. By the sea simmering beyond the wall – the same sea which wore down the fort, and battered the church until it was nothing more than this neat box, and shooshed in the heads of the earliest worshippers. They made the sign of their faith in a place which does not belong entirely to earth but also to air and water; which concentrates the present and makes it ceremonial, but only because it speaks so easily with the past; and which is a rock amidst the currents of this world, while at the same time being a buoyant thing, a coracle afloat on the sense of what is to come.

RIGHT AND ABOVE: The neat "stone barn" church of St Peter-on-the-Wall, one of the oldest churches in England.

Aachen, Germany
AACHEN CATHEDRAL

ABOVE: The choir of Aachen Cathedral with its enormous stained-glass windows. It was added to the original cathedral in the 14th century to accommodate increasing numbers of visiting pilgrims.

RIGHT: The dome of the octagonal Palatine Chapel.

At the heart of Aachen Cathedral rises the Palatine Chapel of Charlemagne, first Holy Roman Emperor. Inside, the octagonal space is small but magnificently decorated. Eastern-inspired striped arches rise from marbled floors to the golden mosaic of the dome. In the dim light, the dome is sometimes partially obscured by clouds of incense released during services. Charlemagne's throne still sits within this masterpiece of Carolingian architecture, a white marble box, positioned so that the king could behold all three altars at once.

The Kaiserdom or the "Imperial Cathedral" has stood in Aachen for more than 1,200 years, making it the oldest cathedral in northern Europe. For centuries, German kings and queens were crowned within its walls. By 800CE Charlemagne's empire stretched across all western Europe and he chose the spa town of Aachen as his seat – the location for his vision of the New Rome.

The architect Odo of Metz created an imitation of San Vitale in Ravenna, incorporating the elements of Byzantine and classical architecture that Charlemagne admired. The chapel was filled with valuable relics, including the four "Great Relics of Aachen": the Virgin Mary's cloak, the infant Jesus' swaddling clothes, Christ's loincloth and the cloth on which John the Baptist's head was laid after his decapitation. So many pilgrims flocked to see these relics (now shown only once every seven years) that in the late 14th century a Gothic choir was added to the cathedral to accommodate them, with thirteen stained-glass windows, each 100 feet (30 metres) high, which flood the choir with coloured light.

Today, Aachen Cathedral sits with quiet grandeur amid the medieval architecture of the old city. Though not as large as the nearby Cologne Cathedral, it retains an unrivalled historical resonance, preserved in its eclectic mix of architectural styles and its museum-worthy collection of relics. But the cathedral is no museum. It is in constant use: every Sunday there is a Latin Mass with Gregorian chants and on Christmas Eve a choir of children sings through the darkness. Aachen remains a living monument to 1,200 years of history, and a spiritual centre for European Christians.

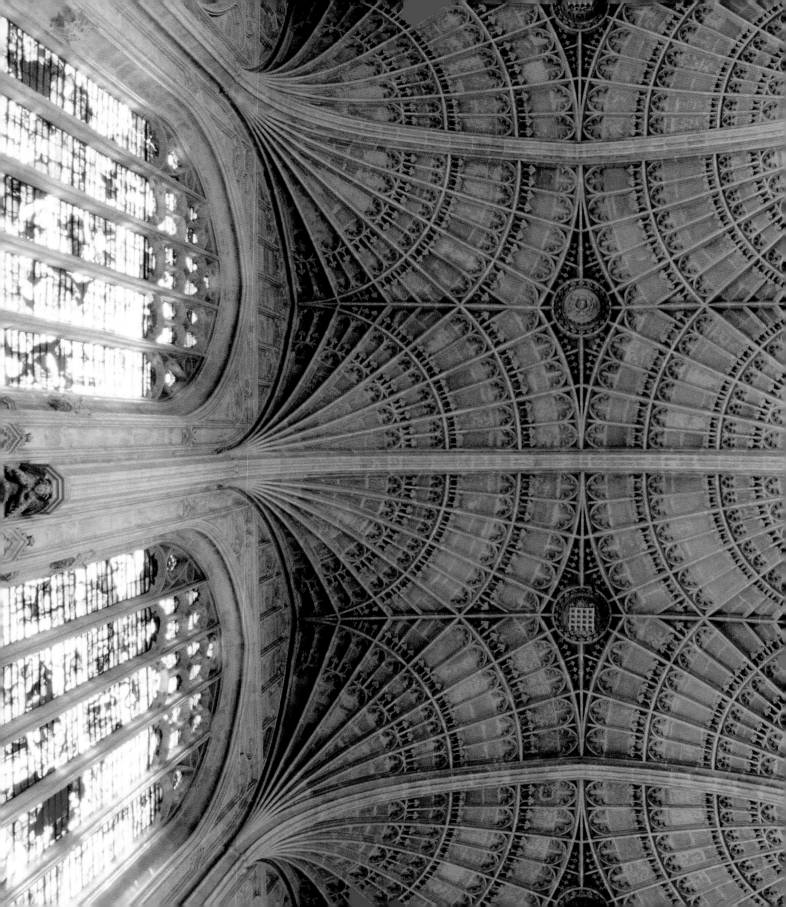

Cambridge, England

KING'S COLLEGE CHAPEL

When he was only nineteen years old, King Henry VI founded King's College and commissioned architect Reginald Ely to design a magnificent chapel for it. Building work began in 1446 and continued over the next 60 years, with two further architects, and funding from kings Edward IV, Richard III, Henry VII and Henry VIII.

The result is a chapel of unparalleled beauty with massive buttresses of pale stone, and corner towers which can be seen for miles across the flatlands of Cambridgeshire. The exterior is impressive, but it is the chapel's lofty interior that takes the breath away. The carved stone roof hovers, seemingly weightless – a fan vault that led Christopher Wren to say that he would build one like it, if any man would tell him where to place the first stone. The antechapel is divided from the choir by a carved oak screen, the gift of Henry VIII, and the chapel is full of Tudor emblems – crowned roses, portcullises and fleurs-de-lys. Rays of sunshine float through the spectacular stained-glass windows, dating mainly from the 16th century, which tell New and Old Testament stories.

It is music, too, that makes the chapel uniquely uplifting. Music was an integral part of the Founder's statutes, which provided for a choir of six adult clerks and sixteen boy choristers. Five hundred years later, King's College choir is famous throughout the world, the voices of the undergraduate choral scholars and boy choristers producing a wonderfully clear, pure sound. The Christmas Eve carol service is broadcast worldwide, but daily evensong is equally beautiful. Boys, who an hour or so before may have been kicking a football, knees still muddy and grazed beneath their cassocks, turn into angels producing ethereal music which, with no amplification, fills the spectacular chapel, its echoes hanging in the air.

LEFT: The soaring fan vault and stained-glass windows depicting New and Old Testament stories inside King's College Chapel, Cambridge.

Menorca, Spain

TALATÍ DE DALT

BY ANDREW MOTION

Mysterious stone remnants that elude understanding

Look at an archaeological map of the Mediterranean: there, in a great scimitar sweep through the western half, lies an extraordinary series of prehistoric sites. Menorca is home to a host of them, as many as 1,600, many set in obscure fields which only farmers visit, well back from the tourist fringe. Even those that have found their way onto popular itineraries still preserve their mystery. The Naveta des Tudons, for instance, a stone funeral-boat, upturned beside the road linking Mao to Ciutadella, and the more elaborate prehistoric village at Talatí de Dalt. For several summers in succession, I took my holidays on the island, and the ancient buildings were my starting point into its strong and stubborn character.

My starting point, and my almost-stopping point too – hard facts are elusive. The period which saw the building of Talatí de Dalt is known as the Talayotic, and flourished between 2000 and 1000 BCE: so far so good. The word *talayot* itself derives from the Arabic word *atalaya*, meaning "watchtower" – but this is puzzling, since it turns out the *talayot*s are circular, square mounds of boulders which might have functioned as tombs, or guard houses, or even homes, as well as look-out posts. Then there are the *taula*s, which consist of two slabs of rock, one balanced on the other to make a "T" shape, and sometimes rising as high as 15 feet (4.5 metres). What were they for? A show of ingenuity and power? Or were they sacrificial altars? Or a means of sky burial? Or the roof supports of buildings which have themselves vanished? Nobody, as the guide books find various ways of saying, "really knows".

But that only whets the appetite. On my last visit I arrived at Talatí de Dalt near sunset, when the site was almost deserted. It was all as I remembered, but entirely strange again. Inside the defensive wall, gigantic sun-whitened stones reared from the boulder-strewn earth – one with a neatly circular hole worn by winter winds and rain. As though a gigantic needle had been stabbed into the ground. Was it chosen because this natural carving made it special – sacred even? There is no way to be sure. Just as there is no way to understand the other slabs rising here and there and everywhere, like remnants of another Stonehenge. And no way either to comprehend the immense *taula*, looming near the centre of the site. When I put my hands against the upright, it breathed like an animal, and was tense with an energy that might suddenly produce fear, or rage, or riot. I sat down, leaning my back against a gnarled hunk of limestone, and waited for darkness to fall. The cicadas wove their orchestras into an endless cloth of sound. Cooling air released the sweet scent of thyme and myrtle. The enormous ghosts drew closer together, circling the silence at their centre, and allowing me to sink down until I was laid flat on their founding simplicity of stone.

LEFT: One of the gigantic *taula*s - "T"-shaped stone structures - at Talatí de Dalt. These megaliths were placed here thousands of years ago during the Talayotic period, and their original purpose remains unclear.

Gourdon, France

ROCAMADOUR

At first glance, the town seems only a crumbling cliff-face of white rock and dark green foliage. But soon, tiny windows, roof tiles and turrets reveal a huddle of beautiful buildings seemingly hewn into the rock and camouflaged against the hillside. Rocamadour is perched high on the steep side of a gorge like a fairytale kingdom, more than 400 feet (120 metres) above the Alzou, a sub-tributary of the Dordogne.

The town's origins are mysterious, and the subject of various myths and legends. It is named after St Amatour, a hermit, whose body was found sealed in a tomb cut into the cliff, and the founder of a shrine there that contained a carved wooden sculpture of a black Madonna. Some claim that St Amatour was in fact Zacchaeus, the tax collector who played host to Jesus on his journey to Jerusalem, and the husband of St Veronica.

To reach the sanctuaries at the top of the hill, the pilgrim must climb a stairway of 216 steps (perhaps on his or her knees, as has been the custom) and follow the winding pathway marked by the stations of the Cross. Among several chapels built into the rock here, the Chapel of Notre Dame is the best known, housing the Madonna, with her infant in her arms and a crown on her head. Votive candles cast light over the shrine, and a great bell, said to have rung of its own accord when prayers were being answered, hangs overhead. An iron sword is embedded in the stone above the chapel entrance, and this, according to tradition, is a fragment of Durandal, the legendary sword of the medieval hero, Roland.

Everywhere, secret stairways wind around corners and beautifully carved balconies, doorways and windows look out across the breathtaking valley. Rocamadour really does seem enchanted in some way, and the precarious splendour of its gravity-defying situation only adds to the impression that the town belongs to another world.

RIGHT: The chapels and houses of Rocamadour, nestled into a gorge above the River Alzou.

County Mayo, Ireland

CROAGH PATRICK

BY JAN MORRIS

To climb as an expression of faith

Even in the Euro-Ireland of the 21st century, so rich, modernist and materialist, holy traditions abound. The priests and nuns of old may not now be so apparent in the streets, but thousands of Irish people still make devout pilgrimages, pause for contemplation at sacred grottoes, cross themselves with water from holy wells or have visionary experiences. All this accumulated faith of the ages, all this congregated numen, seems to me to reach an allegorical epitome at the mountain in County Mayo called Croagh Patrick, or Cruach Phádraig in the Gaelic, and in today's vernacular simply "The Reek".

It is an isolated quartzite cone, 2,500 feet (760 metres) high, magnificently overlooking Clew Bay and its myriad islets, and it was originally known as Cruach Aigil, the Hill of Holy History, because since time immemorial it has been associated with the godly. Druids frequented it long ago, they say, and it was here that St Patrick, during a Lenten fast, not only drove away a host of tormenting demons, but banished serpents from the island once and for all. Various stones and rocks up there are traditionally venerated, and every year, on the last Sunday in July, thousands of people climb the mountain and celebrate a Christian Mass upon its summit.

Christian, Muslim or Jew, atheist or agnostic, you can hardly resist the fervour of this occasion. All through the Saturday night, all day on the Sunday, celebrants labour up the mountain track, some alone, some in groups, some laughing and singing, some reciting Hail Marys to themselves all the way. The weather can be rough at this time of the year in County Mayo, and most of the worshippers are well wrapped up in coats and anoraks, ready for mists, rains and winds on the summit.

There are urchins, priests and pensioners in the crowd, there are rugged old ladies. Teams of soldiers stride the track, and barefoot zealots limp with blood and mud oozing from their toes. Tinkers hang about the path, selling rough-cut sticks – "Reek Sticks" – for if the path seems easy at the bottom, higher up it degenerates into a horribly steep mass of loose shale. They call this "Hell before Heaven", and when I did the climb one year, and we saw this trackless wall of rubble in front of us, stretching away into the mist and rain, even some of the most pious among us were momentarily daunted. "Jesus," a man beside me involuntarily cried, "will you look at that? But never mind," he added, being a merry Irishman, "when we get to the top our souls will be cleaned, and we can start sinning all over again!" So we laughed, gritted our teeth and laboured on up the scree. Sometimes people fell over. Sometimes they just stood still and silent, breathing heavily and praying for help. Now and then stretcher-men stumbled down with casualties, bloodied and bandaged, and we tried not to look at them ...

At the top the pilgrims find Masses being celebrated without pause by teams of priests in a glass-fronted oratory, with the amplified words of the liturgy echoing eerily through the mist, and a tired multitude of devotees milling all around. They have not reached solace yet, though. They must stand in line to make their confessions. They must circumambulate the

RIGHT, ABOVE: Ice and snow near the summit of Croagh Patrick, a common sight in the winter months.

RIGHT, BELOW: Pilgrims making their way up the arduous track to the top of Croagh Patrick on Reek Sunday. Some still climb barefoot. Every year on this day in July, a Christian Mass is celebrated at the summit.

summit fifteen times, reciting the holy texts and sometimes kneeling in prayer. They must make statutory circuits of other mystic sites up there. Only then, after Mass, can they relax with tea and buns at the ad hoc refreshment stands upon the blessed summit.

You may think it a primitive kind of spirituality, and in a way it is. The pilgrims are bruised, breathless and exhausted, pitifully limping around the appointed boulders, murmuring their prayers and fingering their rosaries. But as they sink to the damp turf with their mugs of tea, they are also visibly exhilarated. They are on a high! It has been a voluntarily penitential exercise after all, and that high foggy summit in the wind is a truly holy place. It is holy by heredity, as it were, its holiness inherited from the saints and sages of antiquity, the banishing of snakes and demons, and the centuries of prayer. But it also possesses a grand sanctity of the everyday, perpetuated by those thousands of ordinary people, old and young, year after year, labouring up The Reek with their tinkers' sticks to express their devotion to the divine.

RIGHT: The 2,500 feet (760 metre) high quartzite cone that forms the holy mountain of Croagh Patrick.

Paris, France

SAINTE-CHAPELLE

Standing inside Sainte-Chapelle on a late summer afternoon is like being enclosed inside a towering, jewelled casket. The rays of the sun stream through the soaring stained-glass windows in a flood of multicoloured light and the visitor is bathed in an iridescent glow of red, blue, gold, green and deep mauve.

Since its consecration, in 1248, this delicately-spired Gothic masterpiece has drawn worshippers and admirers alike to the Ile de la Cité. The chapel was commissioned by King Louis IX, as he sought to establish Paris as a western capital of Christendom. Having spent 40,000 *livres* on the chapel's construction, he then paid three times as much on securing holy relics to enshrine here: Christ's crown of thorns, along with some fragments of the Cross.

Today, the relics are gone, scattered during the French Revolution, when the chapel was turned into government offices by Republican rulers keen to erase the country's religious past. Yet the power of the stained glass remains undiminished. There are fifteen impossibly slender windows, 50 feet (15 metres) tall and separated by only the narrowest of stone columns, in accord with the "rayonnant" style of French Gothic architecture, which evolved in the 13th and 14th centuries, and strove for the impression of weightlessness.

Each window tells a sacred Christian story, beginning at the foot of the glass and reading upward from left to right. In all, there are more than 1,000 scenes depicted, showing Christ's childhood, ministry, crucifixion and resurrection. Most spectacular of all is the circular rose window in the west wall; built during the reign of King Charles VIII, in 1485, it depicts the full, tumultuous glory of the Apocalypse.

To feel the might of the setting sun pour through the great rose window is to feel the same awe and wonder that have been experienced by visitors to Sainte-Chapelle for the past seven and a half centuries.

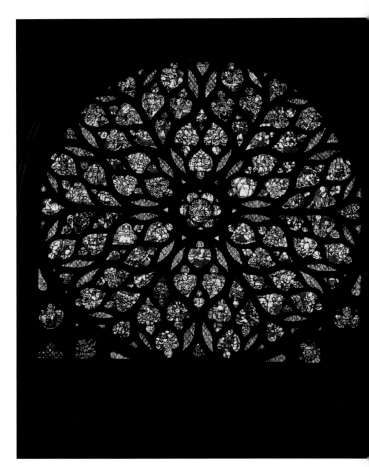

ABOVE: The petal-like forms of the great rose window in Sainte-Chapelle, which was added in the 15th century.

RIGHT: The "jewelbox" interior of the upper chapel, with its spectacular stained-glass windows.

Valaam, Russia

VALAAM MONASTERY

Marooned in the northern waters of Lake Lagonda, between St Petersburg and the Finnish border, the archipelago of Valaam realizes a spiritual ideal of isolation. Remote and tranquil, the monastery that sits on the largest island, also called Valaam, is a haven of piercing beauty under wide, pale northern skies.

So little of the island's history has been recorded that the monastery's origins remain obscure. Some accounts claim that it was founded in the 10th century, others not until the 15th. Most agree, however, that it was established by St Sergius of Valaam, who had travelled here from Greece to this very different archipelago. The climate in this area is harsh, but the temperature on Valaam is a little warmer than on the shores of the lakes. The islands are rocky but green, covered in coniferous forests, and the monks were able to cultivate melons and pumpkins in the monastery gardens.

"Valaam" comes from the Finnish for "high land"; and, standing on the cliffs above the startlingly blue water, the monastery looks as though it might take flight at any moment. The terracotta-pink walls give way to white turrets and ice-blue domes with gold spires reaching heavenward. Pine trees huddle around its edges, cloaking the buildings in dark green.

Inside, the rooms are austere. The black-robed monks, who wear tall hats with long veils attached, are woken at half past three in the morning and pursue a strict routine of prayer and manual labour. With a similar sense of discipline, the *znammeny* chanting for which the monks are famous adheres to an intricate melody that elaborates on a dirge-like drone. The common chants, such as "O gladsome light of Valaam", often speak of the ethereal quality of the light that pervades the islands.

Zelená Hora, Czech Republic

PILGRIMAGE CHURCH OF ST JOHN OF NEPOMUK

There is inspiration to be found in the lives of those prepared to die for their beliefs, for honouring their sacrifice allows us to redefine our own faith. For centuries a pilgrimage to the Church of Saint John of Nepomuk has helped Roman Catholics in eastern Europe move closer to God.

In the 14th century St John was hurled from the Charles Bridge in Prague into the turbulent river below. When his drowned body was found washed up on the bank, a vision of a crown with five stars appeared in the air above him. For 400 years his tongue was miraculously preserved as a macabre relic. The Pope declared the tongue to be incorruptible evidence of John's sainthood; and work on the church at Zelená Hora, or Green Hill, began.

Built into the side of the hill, a long flight of stairs leads up to one of the most splendid and original churches in Europe. The sunlight stretches the flickering shadows of trees across the gleaming white cemetery walls. These walls zig-zag around the church forming a decagon. At equal distances along the wall are ten red-roofed towers.

Above each of the five entrance gates is a gilt star and inside the walls sits a star-shaped church with five altars, the main one featuring five stars and five angels. The Prague architect Jan Santini built the church using the star and the number five repeatedly in the layout and proportions of his structure, echoing the vision that appeared above the dead St John.

Much as a Roman Catholic counts the beads of a rosary to focus in prayer, the symbolic and numerical references to St John's life embedded in the church's design focus the pilgrim's mind upon the nature of martyrdom and what it really means to have the courage to live according to one's convictions.

Teutoburger Wald, Germany

EXTERNSTEINE

At the top of a towering limestone crag, reached by precarious stone steps and a narrow footbridge, is a tiny and now roofless sanctuary that was hewn from the rock many centuries ago. A circular hole bored through the eastern wall of this sanctuary looks down on the forest below. On one morning in the year, midsummer's day, the rays of the rising sun pass through the hole and strike brightly against the far wall, illuminating what was once a shrine, where a Christian altar in the form of a low pillar still stands.

The crag is called the Sternwarte, the "Observatory", and is one of the Externsteine, a group of five sheer pillars of limestone that rise as high as 120 feet (37 metres) above the Teutoburger Forest near Detmold in northwest Germany. Stone Age peoples came to this sombre and haunting place as far back as 10,000BCE. So too, it was once believed, did worshippers of Odin and other Germanic gods, though nothing has ever been found to prove this conclusively.

But the rocks were a holy place long before the first Christian hermits came here around 1,000 years ago. The sanctuary on the Sternwarte, with its hole for observing the summer solstice sunrise (and the most northerly moonrise), was in existence long before Christian monks turned it into a chapel. Ancient visitors hewed dark chambers and tunnels in the rock, bored holes and depressions whose purpose is now a mystery, and carved stone steps that seem to go nowhere.

At the base of one of the rocks is a monumental relief of Christ being taken down from the Cross, carved ca. 1150 and unique in northern European Romanesque art. Among the details of this magnificent relief is a dragon – the symbol of the devil and of paganism – whose might was broken by Christ's sacrifice. The image no doubt reflects the awesome powers once ascribed to these extraordinary stones.

LEFT: The natural limestone pillars of the Externsteine have been ascribed sacred importance since the Stone Age. The tallest of the pillars is now home to a Christian chapel.

Galicia, Spain

SANTIAGO DE COMPOSTELA

BY JAN MORRIS

A holy road to fulfilment

Any day of the year on the roads of northern Spain you may see walkers making for the northwestern province of Galicia – bundled in scarves and raincoats in winter, sweating in the summer sun, but unmistakable, almost one and all, for their air of cheerful determination.

They are on their way to one of the holiest places of Christianity, Santiago de Compostela – Saint James of the Field of a Star. There, holy legend says, the remains of St James the Apostle lie in his tomb, his sarcophagus having been miraculously transported from Jerusalem, and its site revealed by the eponymous star. For centuries Christian pilgrims from many countries have made their way to his shrine within one of the most festively remarkable of all cathedrals.

There is nothing penitential to this splendid church. It seems to summon its pilgrims not to repentance, but to benediction. When they get there at last, theirs will be the joy of a hard journey completed in a noble spirit, and the building seems designed to offer them congratulatory welcomes. It stands on an elevation above a ceremonial square, and even in Santiago's notoriously dismal weather it seems to be all a golden glow. Its tremendous façade and its three tall granite towers are extravagantly carved with pinnacles and crevices, bells, stars, figures of the Apostle, figures of attendant saints, figures of the Almighty, in a sensational outburst of sacred ornament. It is the most exuberant of holy buildings!

The pilgrims enter it by way of a grand double-staircase off the square, and through a gloriously opulent doorway. Almost at once, if they are of traditional instincts, they will pay homage to the creator of the doorway, the 12th-century architect Master Mateo. He is supposed to be the figure

ABOVE: The densely carved Baroque façade of Santiago de Compostela, added to the cathedral in the 17th century.

LEFT: The famous Pórtico da Gloria, composed of some 200 figures sculpted by Master Mateo in the 12th century.

sculpted in a kneeling position at the foot of a pillar, and the accepted ritual is to bump one's brow against his forehead, and thus obtain a little of his inspiration.

Then up the great nave of the building, at the shrine behind the high altar, comes the supreme moment of the Santiago experience, passing through the crypt that houses the saintly relics, and embracing a 13th-century image of St James himself – a moment of such ecstasy for the faithful that many a pilgrim is reduced to tears of gratitude.

It was all worth it, they seem to be saying then – all those hundreds of dusty miles to reach this climax of Christian dedication. No matter that many of those pilgrims are not really Christians at all, but have made the journey merely to prove themselves, or just for the adventure of it. No matter that the meaning of "Compostela", theorists now maintain, is nothing to do with stars. No matter even that in historical fact St James does not lie in that cathedral at all, and never came near the place.

No matter! The pilgrimage to the Field of the Star has been given true sanctity by the generations of the Christian faithful who have undertaken it, and the shrine of its destination breathes a sacred spirit of fulfilment.

RIGHT: The huge barrel-vaulted nave, leading to the high altar. Side aisles and an ambulatory around the apse were included in the design to facilitate the movement of large numbers of pilgrims.

BELOW: The relics of St James are kept in the crypt, below the high altar. Down here one can appreciate the scale of the original modest 9th-century church around which the cathedral was built and expanded upon until the 18th century.

Norway

AURORA BOREALIS

In one of the earliest accounts of the aurora borealis or "Northern Lights", in the 1230 Norse chronicle *Konungs skuggsjá*, the writer struggles to explain this mesmerizing phenomenon. Perhaps flares from the other side of the Earth had reached around to the night sky? Perhaps glaciers were full of pent-up energy escaping into the atmosphere? Or perhaps the vast icy oceans of the North were surrounded by fires, whose licks of flame could be dimly seen through the darkness.

Today, we know that the lights are caused by charged oxygen and nitrogen particles, carried from the sun's surface on the solar wind, crashing into our atmosphere and exploding. Still, even with this scientific understanding, we can never say precisely when these luminous wisps of green, red and blue, which seem to dissolve in the sky as if a stained-glass window had been tinted with watercolour, will appear. Little wonder, then, that the aurora borealis – named by Galileo in the 17th century for the Roman goddess of dawn and the Greek term for the North Wind – continues to inspire awestruck humility.

People travel from all over the world to the locations closest to the North Magnetic Pole (one of two points on Earth where the magnetic field is vertical), such as the far north of Canada, Greenland, Iceland and Scandinavia, where the lights are most often seen. Changes in the Earth's core mean that this pole is gradually moving; currently it is located near Ellesmere Island in northern Canada. In September and October, and March and April, the vernal and autumnal equinoxes make the diffractions of colour most likely to materialize. Nevertheless, however much one pays for a guided cruise, or a hike to the darkest parts of the Arctic Circle, the lights remain tantalizingly unpredictable.

RIGHT: The aurora borealis as seen from northern Norway. These dazzling colours are actually photon emissions from charged particles, excited by the particles carried in the solar wind and accelerated by the Earth's magnetic field.

Metéora, Greece

ROUSANOU MONASTERY

RIGHT: Rousanou is one of six monastries still in use at Metéora (meaning "rocks in the air"). The buildings are set in sandstone cliffs and range from between 700 and 2,000 feet (200 and 600 metres) high. Hermits have been living in this remote area since the 9th century.

Metéora is a landscape of towering peaks eroded into epic stone pillars of biblical dimensions. Perched precariously atop one of the columns of rock, with cliffs dropping off sharply on every side, Rousanou monastery keeps watch over the landscape below. With its red roof tiles glinting warmly in the sunlight, Rousanou seems to be placed somewhere between heaven and Earth.

The first people to live on these inhospitable pinnacles were determined hermits who climbed up to caves and fissures in the rock and set up lives of solitude intended for the contemplation of God. Eventually they came together to form monasteries. During the lawlessness of the Ottoman invasions in the 14th and 15th centuries, the monks found themselves moving higher and higher up the sheer cliffs, seeking protection in inaccessibility.

Originally the only mode of access to Rousanou was in a large net hauled up the cliff by the monks above. According to the local people these ropes were not replaced until "the Lord let them break". This ensured that only the most pious of pilgrims would attempt the journey. Today there are steps and a wooden bridge. Having ascended to the monastery, the visitor enters into an atmosphere of intense holiness that has attracted the devout for more than 500 years. The complex is made up of a small church and cells built around a central courtyard. The interior of the church is decorated with frescoes depicting the Assumption of the Virgin, Christ's resurrection, and the martyrdoms of the saints in all their gory brilliance. The enormity of effort it must have taken to build this monument of faith is overwhelming. Here, the modern world quite literally falls away and all that remains as you look up are the wood and stone buildings of the courtyard framing an ocean of sky.

Tomar, Portugal

CONVENTO DE CRISTO

The significance of the Convento de Cristo is at least partly due to its value as a symbol of Portugal's changing relationship with the world. The Convento was originally a castle built in the 12th century on a hill near the river Nabao. Constructed by the Knights Templar, it was designed as part of a wall of defence against the infidel Moors. The oldest part of the present-day complex is the rotunda, or *charola* in Portuguese, which was built around this time. Shafts of light stream in from windows set high in the walls, illuminating the richly decorated interior with its painted statues of saints and angels. Even the curved ceiling is covered in paintings depicting the lives of Christ and his apostles.

In the 14th century the Knights Templar regrouped as the Order of Christ, whose considerable wealth was used to expand their headquarters at Tomar. An ornate nave was added to the complex, with carvings as delicate and complicated as lacework. The famous west window of the Chapter House is covered in sculpture so dense and intricate that it is difficult to discern the subject matter at first. Gradually details emerge – ropes now covered with lichen that makes them look as though they have just been hauled from the briny depths, sails billowing, mariners at work and impressive seascapes – all iconic symbols of a rich nautical heritage. The 15th century was Portugal's great age of discovery. Ships left Portuguese ports, headed down the African coast and came back laden with gold that made Portugal rich.

As a result the Convento was transformed from a stronghold that shut out the world to a gallery resplendent with the riches found in exploration.

LEFT: Hundreds of paintings and sculptures adorn the interior of the 12th-century *charola* or rotunda, the oldest part of the Convento de Cristo.

near Kinloch, Scotland

MORVERN

BY ALEXANDER McCALL SMITH

A remote landscape, touched by past sorrows and spirituality

Morvern is one of the least populated parts of Scotland. Prior to the Highland Clearances, the dark tragedy that befell the people of the north and west of Scotland in the 18th and 19th centuries, there were over 2,000 people living in this remote, mountainous region. Now it is a fraction of that, and many square miles of heart-breakingly beautiful countryside are devoid of any sign of human life. Yet the traces of people who have disappeared from the land are never entirely obliterated.

I recall reading William Dalrymple's account of his travels through land previously occupied by Palestinians in which he saw, beneath the new works on the land, the old boundaries stubbornly reappearing – hedge-plants that had been boundaries for dispossessed farmers coming up through the soil, their roots not entirely eradicated, to remind us of the people who had been there before. Whatever the rights and wrongs of that tragic conflict – and both sides can marshal their claims – it is nonetheless true that to lose one's land makes a very particular wound in the soul. And that happened to many Scots, for whom exile to Canada or the United States was the only option. In this case, those who left were perhaps more fortunate than those who stayed – the sense of loss was keener at home, perhaps, amongst the people who saw the numbers of those who spoke their language, sang their Gaelic songs, knew their genealogy, dwindle.

Morvern, then, is a place of loss, a place where a whole culture became fragile and stumbled, perhaps fatally. So, just as the old hedges may struggle up in the Holy Land, here and there on the hills in this part of Scotland one comes across houses long since tumbled into ruins; sheep enclosures, lovingly built of stone, now mere mounds in the earth; places where boats were kept, fish smoked and cured,

paths where barefoot children walked long miles to tiny schools. All of these have gone.

Yet the spiritual power of this landscape remains, and, curiously enough, it is this spirituality that still draws people to this land and contributes to its regeneration. People choose to live here now because of the quiet pace of life, the lack of stress, the sheer affecting beauty of these hills and lochs.

Everywhere one is reminded of the spiritual past. The iconoclastic severity of the Scottish Reformation may have left Scotland's churches with a style that is cold and unadorned, and yet there are many reminders of a time when Scotland was rich in colourful saints. Not far from Morvern is the holy island of Iona, where St Columba brought Christianity from Ireland. Many people visit Iona today to experience its strong sense of the spiritual, but one does not have to go to Iona to be reminded of the early Scottish saints – one only has to look at the map to see the place names commemorating their doings. Ben Hiant, "Holy Mountain" in Gaelic, can be viewed from the far end of Loch Teacuis. At the foot of this mountain St Columba was said to have stepped ashore and found a holy well. The mountain looks out to Coll and Tiree and the Outer Hebrides beyond. It is a place of soft mists and poetry and ancient saints who knew – as we know today – that they were on the edge of darkness.

LEFT: Looking across Loch Linne toward the sparsely populated rocky landscape of Morvern.

FOLLOWING PAGES: The gentle snow-clad peaks of Ben Hiant (Gaelic for "Holy Mountain") in wintertime.

Uppsala, Sweden

GAMLA UPPSALA

Gamla Uppsala, home of the kings, dwelling place of gods and temple of human sacrifice. The name has become synonymous with ancient Swedish paganism. Today, pilgrims can still see the rolling green mounds of the 1,700-year-old Swedish burial site, just outside the university town of Uppsala, but they may find it difficult to understand the significance of the pagan rituals that were performed here.

By the Iron Age, the water that once covered the land here had receded and burials began to be performed, resulting in thousands of barrow downs, of which 250 remain – curious emerald humps in the lowland landscape. The kings who lived at Uppsala were given grand burial ceremonies according to the laws of the god Odin – their bodies burned to transport their souls to Valhalla. The remains were then buried along with weapons and riches under great mounds of earth, the "barrows". Consequently, as well as being a place of spiritual significance, Uppsala is an archaeological treasure trove.

The site was one of the last strongholds of pagan Germanic kingship. By 1070, after most of Sweden had been converted to Christianity, the chronicler Adam of Bremen wrote of a pagan civilization with ferocious rituals that involved human sacrifices in a sacred grove. Adam also described an ornate temple, surrounded by trees and encircled by a golden chain draped around its gables. Inside was the triple throne of Thor, Odin and Freyr.

Today, an 11th-century church (*above*) stands on top of what are probably the foundations of the original temple. The church was once a large cathedral, but its nave and transepts were destroyed by fire, leaving behind the present-day modest stone structure. Eventually, Christianity would engulf the old religion of Uppsala's first inhabitants, but even in this sombre little church, with its heavy crucifixes and religious sculptures, one can sense an even more ancient and mysterious spirituality.

Turku, Finland

TURKU CATHEDRAL

At noon each day, Finnish radio broadcasts a sound that resonates in the heart of every Finn: the chiming of the bells of Turku Cathedral. The city of Turku – also called Åbo by its Swedish-speaking minority – was the capital of Finland for centuries before the Russian Empire annexed the country in 1814 and moved the capital to Helsinki, which was closer to Russia. Turku retains a special place in Finnish culture as home to a 700-year-old cathedral, the seat of the Finnish Lutheran church and a revered symbol of national self-esteem. The cathedral is also the country's national shrine, and the burial place of many famous Finns.

Entering the nave, you have a sense that the cathedral is at once ancient and modern. Its interior evokes both Protestant piety, in its plain walls, which support the massive Gothic vaults, and medieval Catholicism, in its brightly coloured fragments of saintly frescoes, such as St Barbara

surrounded by delicate foliage and St Veronica holding her famous veil imprinted with Christ's image. Two statues of the 1400s are moving in their exquisite skill and profound humanity: one portrays the Virgin and Child in the arms of St Anne; the other, the grieving Mary cradling the crucified body of Jesus.

During the Reformation, many of the statues and images of saints and other Catholic furnishings were stored out of sight in the sacristy – where they later survived the Great Fire of 1827, which devastated the cathedral and destroyed most of the city. You can still see fire-blackened bricks on the church tower, below the rebuilt steeple. Inside, the 19th-century restoration bore such impressive fruits as Fredrik Westin's Neo-Gothic altarpiece and Carl Ludwig Engel's gilded pulpit, which together form a striking counterpoint to the cathedral's plain Gothic grandeur.

ABOVE AND RIGHT: The wooden materials of Sogn Benedetg New Chapel reflect its forested surroundings. This intimate chapel stands on a steep slope and has a teardrop plan that makes the building look circular, oval or like the keel of a boat depending on the angle from which it is viewed.

Sumvitg, Switzerland

SOGN BENEDETG NEW CHAPEL

The village of Sogn Benedetg – the local Romansch language translation of "St Benedict" – stands high in the Swiss Alps with spectacular views of the valley below. Its tranquillity was abruptly shattered in 1984, when an avalanche destroyed the old 13th-century chapel (*chaplutta*) that stood on higher ground just west of the village. The new chapel, by Swiss architect Peter Zumthor, was completed in 1988 on a different site to the north. Built of wood rather than the traditional stone of its ruined predecessor, the chapel is also radically innovative in form. It has a teardrop plan that has been described as evoking a boat, a leaf, or an eye – presumably the all-seeing eye of God.

While unequivocally modern, the *chaplutta* is in profound harmony both with its setting and with ancient Christian spiritual traditions. Its bells hang from a pylon-like structure which stands next to the building itself. The chapel therefore has no spire, but is designed so that it doesn't need one: seen from the village below, the entire building looks like a cylindrical tower, connecting heaven and Earth.

The ceiling tapers toward the altar end of the chapel, naturally drawing the view of the congregation heavenward, as does the chapel's unbroken ring of windows, set high up, like a traditional clerestory.

At first sight the interior, with its striking beamed ceiling like an upturned boat, may not resemble a conventional church nave. But the word "nave" literally means "ship", denoting the space as a "vessel of souls". The chapel is a place of safety and refuge from the stormy seas of life, where people can come together for worship and prayer, or simply for peace and contemplation.

Devon, England

WISTMAN'S WOOD

BY ANDREW MOTION

Precious survivor of wild nature

Wistman's Wood: it feels as remote as the name sounds strange. In the middle of Dartmoor and associated with ancient Druidic rites, this is one of wild nature's most precious survivors.

I drive close to the centre of the moor, leave the car in the yard of a shadowy hotel at Two Bridges, pull up my collar, then clamber over a gate and head up the valley of the West Dart river. There is no sign to the wood, but a friend had told me not to miss it. Here on my left is the farm he mentioned, with chickens bobbing in the yard and a seething black dog on a leash. To the right and ahead, the moor slowly releases its mist-sighs, opening wider and wider to catch the sprinkles of lark-song. What was I expecting to find? I know the facts alright. Dartmoor used to be covered in forest, apart from the highest tors, then at the end of the Mesolithic and during the Neolithic, people cleared it for farming, creating the wilderness we know. In a very few places the ancient woodland survives, and nowhere more hauntingly than here. Or so my friend has told me, describing

a tangle of stunted oaks, with a few rowan, holly and willow trees, writhing from moss-covered boulders and draped with mosses, lichens and fern.

I walk for a good hour, the wet air shining me, then come face to face with the wood. It is like nothing I have seen before. In the earliest records, everyone concentrates on the shrivelled, wind-blasted scale. The trees are "no taller than a man may touch to top with his head," said Tristram Risdon in 1620. Centuries of effort have stretched them a little – as I begin to circle, I see specimens as tall as 20 feet (6 metres).

BELOW: The ancient, stunted oak trees of Wistman's Wood, cloaked in lichen and moss. According to legend the grove was sacred to the Druids and they performed pagan rituals here.

But these are exceptions. Most are no bigger than I am, with skinny, silvery-green arms and hands twisted around the invisible fingers of air. Living is such a gigantic effort! That is what their gestures say. Look at what we have to manage on: flying rain-drops and mist in the air, and boulders where there should be earth! And the boulders are immense – as massive, in fact, as the trees are small, so the entire wood is a complicated trick of scale. The longer I stare, the more evidently it becomes a bewitchment: Wistman's is an adaptation of Wisht Hounds, the Devonshire dialect term for the hellhounds which pursue sinners and the unbaptised.

I complete my circle, then cover my face with my hands and press forward. The wood shudders, feathery branches lunging at me to wipe their lichens across my eyes and mouth. I immediately come to a standstill. My entry is a violation, nothing more. Anyway, what did I want? Some sense of the centre? The centre is impenetrable – a slowly-churning riot of wood and leaf and fibre that makes its own world and needs nothing from me. That rejects me, in fact. Drives me back into the spinning air where, after a minute of striving, I stand still and breathing heavily. I am an onlooker, expelled from the overgrown garden. It is my fate and consolation to bow my head, then begin the long tramp back across the moor to where I began.

RIGHT AND LEFT: Moss, lichen and ferns cover almost every surface in the wood.

Assisi, Italy

BASILICA OF ST FRANCIS

The sheer scale of this hilltop complex indicates the reverence in which St Francis was held throughout the Christian world. In the early 13th century, having experienced a religious conversion, Francis abandoned his soldierly ambitions, and started writing spiritual poetry. In his works he put forward the notion that the best way to gaze upon the divine was to contemplate the wonders of God's creation, as manifested in plant and animal life. It was on this philosophy, and the virtues of penitence and abstinence, that he founded the monastic order of which this basilica is the mother church.

The elevated stone edifice of St Francis' Basilica still dominates the surrounding countryside, as it has for seven and a half centuries. It is divided into two sections, upper and lower, and its half-Gothic, half-Romanesque bulk seems to soar upward out of the majestic hilltop friary that housed the monks who came to join the Order of St Francis.

Enter via the lower basilica, and you pass beneath the ornate rose window, the "church's eye". Above you are the bright, open spaces of the upper basilica, below you the crypt housing St Francis' tomb. For many years, the saint's last resting-place was kept a secret, to prevent his remains from being distributed piecemeal across Europe, as holy relics.

The glory of the Basilica's interior lies not in the stained-glass windows that pierce its walls at regular intervals, but in the artworks that surround them. Frescoes by artists such as Cimabue and Giotto illustrate St Francis' vision of man and nature in harmony. Rather than trumpeting the might of the church, the Basilica celebrates the quiet virtues of humility and kindness.

RIGHT: The Basilica of St Francis is set on a hillside on the outskirts of Assisi. Built to house the remains and commemorate the life of St Francis, the Basilica is the mother church of the Franciscan monastic order.

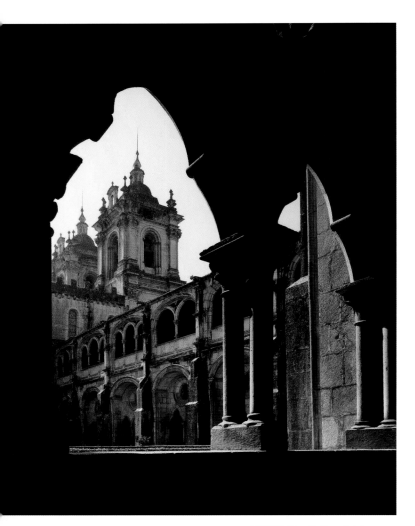

ABOVE: The Gothic cloister, known as the Cloister of Silence, added to Alcobaça Abbey by King Dinis I in the 13th century.

RIGHT: A view down the soaring, narrow nave of the abbey from behind the high altar. Ornament was kept to a minimum in keeping with the principles of Cistercian architecture.

Alcobaça, Portugal

ALCOBAÇA ABBEY

The abbey of St Mary of Alcobaça was founded in 1153 by Afonso Henriques (1139–85), the first king of Portugal, in the wake of independence from León and a string of victories against Iberia's Muslim rulers. Afonso granted the site to the Cistercian order which had been recently founded by St Bernard, and the monastery emulated Bernard's own great abbey at Clairvaux in France. Today Clairvaux stands in ruins, but we can still view Alcobaça in all its medieval glory, the first example of pure Gothic architecture in Portugal and unsurpassed anywhere in Europe for the sheer scale and beauty of its construction. Consecrated in 1252, it remains the largest church in Portugal.

The main façade of the monastery, remodelled in the Baroque era, does little to prepare you for the impact of the interior. Stepping through the west door, visitors invariably catch their breath. The nave is high and long, but narrow – at 71 feet (22 metres), its width is less than a fifth of its length – and this creates a soaring effect that immediately raises the eyes, and the spirit, to the heavens. The overwhelming impression is one of monumental simplicity, with only the simplest carving on the columns as decoration. For St Bernard, the monastery was a place to enrich the soul, not the body, a holy place where the inner life took precedence over outward forms, and Cistercian architecture reflected this ideal, as at Sénanque Abbey in France (*see pp40–41*).

The interior is by no means gloomy, however, because its pale stone is illuminated by large windows, including a great rose window at the western end. There are also rose windows in both transepts, where legendary tragic lovers King Pedro I and Inês de Castro lie in intricately carved marble tombs that contrast with the plainness of the surrounding masonry.

The abbey church is a place of solemn majesty, where unshakable faith is expressed in solid stone. The adjacent Cloister of Silence has a similar exquisite simplicity, but is more delicate in scale and execution. The impact is less majestic but more intimate, befitting a place where monks once paced in silent contemplation.

Tuscany, Italy

MONTALCINO & THE ABBEY OF SANT'ANTIMO

BY ALEXANDER McCALL SMITH

Landscape of timeless harmony

I first went to Montalcino when I was a student at the University of Siena – the places one visits when young can make a lasting impression, rendered all the more powerful by the passage of time and by the way that memory blurs details. I took a bus that climbed up the winding road to the small town, disembarking near the forbidding fortress that dominates all approaches. In those days there were fewer visitors, and the prevailing atmosphere was one of somnolence. As is the case with many Italian towns and villages, there was a strong sense that important things had happened here, but only a very long time ago. I spent a day exploring the town's alleys and the paths that meandered around the slopes of the surrounding olive groves. At virtually every point one is afforded a view of Tuscan countryside that must surely have been the backdrop to a hundred Renaissance paintings. Had angels appeared in the empty skies above those hills it would have been no surprise – just as an angelic flight was no surprise to Al Alvarez in his touching poem "Angels in Italy", composed in just such surroundings.

On my next visit, years later, I made forays into the surrounding countryside. I walked to Sant'Angelo in Colle, a hill village which, when viewed from a distance, seemed to be floating in the sky, detached from the land below. I passed a farmyard with two white oxen and a rickety wooden cart parked under a tree. There was no sense of urgency, no sense that earning a living from the land in such surroundings was a battle; there was a strong feeling of complete and timeless harmony.

And then I discovered the Abbey of Sant'Antimo, just a few miles south of the town. This is widely regarded as the most beautiful of Italian Romanesque churches, a building of soft feminine shape, with a perfect square tower, and surrounded by cypress trees and olive groves. Spirituality can grow with age: a place of prayer, as this place is, acquires what one might describe as a spiritual patina. Hundreds of years of monastic chant seem to have penetrated the very fabric of this abbey, reminding us of the ancient roots of our Western religious traditions. It does not matter if the visitor cannot accept the literal truth of what is proclaimed here: what really counts is the expression of spiritual yearning that has made this place holy to the monks and ordinary people who have worshipped in this building over the centuries.

The ancient offices are still told here: lauds, terce, sext, none, vespers, compline. The regularity of the religious timetable reflects the regularity of the seasons and life in the surrounding Tuscan countryside. Do not hurry. Olives and grapes ripen in their own time. Stop and listen. Contemplate who you are and why you are doing what you are doing. Close your eyes. Imagine angels.

PREVIOUS PAGES, LEFT:
The rolling low hills of the
Orcia Valley, which surrounds
Montalcino.

PREVIOUS PAGES, RIGHT:
The clustered buildings of the
medieval hilltown of Montalcino.
The town was named for a type
of oak tree that once grew in
the area.

LEFT: The Abbey of Sant'Antimo,
set among the cypress trees and
olive groves typical of this part
of Tuscany. It was built for the
most part in the 12th century. Its
smooth contours and rounded
arches are characteristic of
Romanesque architecture.

Djenné, Mali

THE GREAT MOSQUE

At first sight the uneven surfaces and conical spires of the Great Mosque of Djenné give this astonishing building the appearance of a giant termite mound, indistinguishable in substance and colour from the red-brown earth on which it stands. The spires adorn an Islamic place of worship but they belong to a much older spiritual tradition, as can be seen in the shrines of Mali's Dogon people, which honour earth gods and ancestor spirits (*see pp126–9*). At the Great Mosque, the tallest spires crown the three minarets on the eastern façade – the side facing Mecca – and are each surmounted by an ostrich egg, a traditional symbol of life, fertility and renewal. At Djenné, the sanctity of an Islamic holy space is intimately bound to an ancient reverence for the earth and – in a region uneasily positioned on the fringe of the barren Sahara – its precarious fertility.

The Great Mosque is the world's largest building constructed of adobe – bricks of dried mud and straw plastered over with a coat of mud. Built on an artificial platform well above the level of any floods, it towers over Djenné's market square, with walls 245 feet (75 metres) long and 65 feet (20 metres) high. Two prayer halls take up half the mosque's area, the other half being an open courtyard. The mud walls help to cool the dark interior of the main prayer hall, where up to a thousand worshippers can pray on mats among a forest of wooden pillars that support the roof.

Although the mosque is protected from floods, its mud walls are still vulnerable to rain and the year-round searing heat. Waterspouts direct rain well away from the mosque, while the walls bristle with palm branches that help to absorb the stresses caused by variations in temperature and humidity. These branches also serve as ladders when, once a year, the entire population of Djenné descends on the mosque with buckets of mud to make essential repairs to the exterior. For a people so dependent on the soil, it is a fitting act of gratitude to Allah for his continued blessings.

ABOVE: A shadowy passageway inside the Great Mosque.

RIGHT: A glimpse of the three great towers on the eastern façade. The dark protrusions are bundles of palm branches.

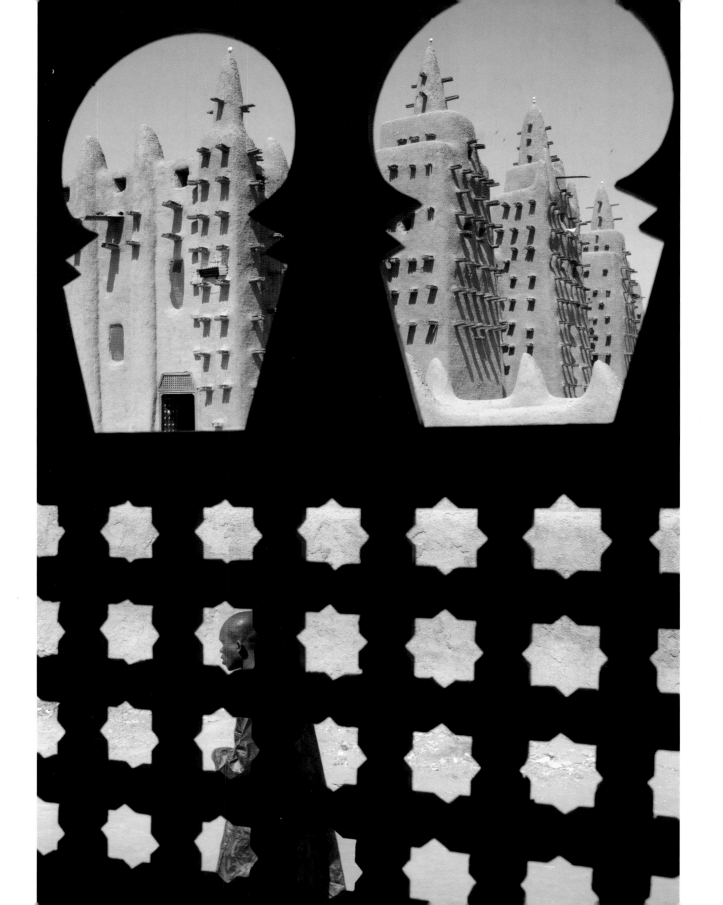

Bethlehem Municipality, West Bank

BETHLEHEM

Bethlehem is many different things to many different people. It means Christ's birthplace, a little town with an inn and a manger. It means barbed wire and a hated wall, and a church under siege. It means Christendom's crusader kings, and a Muslim majority in Palestine. It means trinkets for tourists and relics for pilgrims. It means, literally, "House of Bread" if you return to the old Hebrew, or "House of Meat" if you trust the original Arabic. The infertile desert on the doorstep seems to scoff at both those translations. This is a hard town to know.

It is, however, decidedly worth making the effort. A busy community of 30,000 people, Bethlehem, sited at the heart of some of history's oldest disputes, has not always been a happy part of the world, but it has always been a crucial one.

For Christians, of course, this is the scene of Christ's nativity, a significance commemorated by the imposing Church of the Nativity. Set over a grotto where the Virgin Mary is said to have given birth to Jesus, knocked down, rebuilt, conquered, retaken, even besieged by Israeli forces when Palestinian militants took refuge there in 2002, it is now controlled jointly by three Christian denominations, and is still the main attraction for the hundreds of thousands of visitors to the city. For Jews, too, the town is an important destination for pilgrimage, and many come every year to visit the tomb of Rachel, Jacob's wife and the "eternal mother".

For the town's population, Bethlehem is a home before anything else, and the wall that separates the town from Israel is a common cause of distress to Muslim inhabitants, who make up the majority, and to the ancient Christian community – whose gradual exodus has been attributed by many to the barrier. Despite its associations with political contention, however, Bethlehem retains an atmosphere of reverence that is repected by Christians, Jews and Muslims alike.

ABOVE: The interior of the Church of the Nativity in Manger Square, Bethlehem. An important site for both Christians and Muslims, and the location of a dramatic siege in 2002, the church is built over a cave thought to be the birthplace of Jesus.

LEFT: The Bethlehem skyline. Two church spires flank the minaret of the Mosque of Omar, the only mosque in the old town.

Sinai Peninsula, Egypt

MOUNT SINAI

Mount Sinai does not claim to be the highest mountain in the South Sinai region, nor even the most spectacular. The mountain's significance is rooted in something far stronger: belief.

For Christians, this is the mountain where God spoke to Moses: here Moses received the Ten Commandments, was given his mission from God and came across the Burning Bush. While there is some controversy over whether the modern-day Mount Sinai is in fact the same location as the biblical Mount Sinai, pilgrims still flock to climb this sacred mountain by way of a steep track known as the Sikket Saydna Musa, the "Path of Moses", which climbs up 3,750 "steps of penitence".

At the foot of the mountain is St Catherine's monastery – one of the oldest functioning Christian monasteries in the world. According to legend, the remains of the martyred St Catherine of Alexandria were transported to Mount Sinai by angels and discovered by monks. The monastery, which sits at the mouth of an inaccessible gorge, is today a popular pilgrimage site in its own right and houses the world's second largest collection of early codices and manuscripts.

Starting in the middle of the night to avoid the heat, pilgrims climb in the dark, past cypress trees, ancient chapels and structures honouring saints and the Virgin Mary, and a stone arch where, long ago, a monk is reputed to have sat and heard the confessions of passers-by. Nearing the summit, they encounter a natural amphitheatre where the 70 wise men waited while God spoke to Moses. At the rocky summit there is a mosque and a small Greek Orthodox chapel. Here, pilgrims pray and offer thanks, or simply gaze into the airy distances as the sun rises over the surrounding mountains.

LEFT: Pilgrims praying at the spot where God is supposed to have spoken to Moses on Mount Sinai.

Damascus, Syria

UMAYYAD MOSQUE   BY JAN MORRIS

In the sacred compound

In the tumultuous heart of Damascus – a kaleidoscopic spectacle of traffic and crowds, all motion, all bustle, every variety of face, colour and noise – at one end of the seething bazaars there stands an enclave of indisputable holiness.

The Great Mosque of the Umayyads at Damascus is the oldest of all the major ceremonial mosques of Islam, and for many centuries the site has been celebrated for its sanctity. Once there was a Roman temple here, dedicated to the god Jupiter. For years there was a Christian cathedral, in which the supposed head of the martyred John the Baptist was venerated. When it became a Muslim mosque in the 9th century, its builders consciously set out to make it a wonder of the Islamic world.

We are told that the very first progenitor of all mosques was hardly more than a roofless ground-plan scratched in the Arabian sands, until buildings arose to commemorate Muhammad's own mud-brick compound in Medina. So to this day the Great Mosque at Damascus possesses elements of the austere and the domestic, the whole evolved into a prodigy of noble conviction.

Part of it is a great pillared and carpeted prayer hall, shadowy and suggestive, and there among the serried columns, at any hour of the day, the faithful sit, pray and meditate, shaded against the Syrian heat, in a tremendous reincarnation of that mud enclosure in Medina long ago. The rest of the mosque, though, is open to the sky, and in its immense colonnaded quadrangle one may fancy that roofless square in the sand where the first of all the Muslims prayed to Allah – an immense stark enclosure once decorated with vibrant mosaics, now mostly monochrome and severe, like a patch of desert itself. Pigeons fly around, people wander here and there or sit about quietly thinking.

And high above that spectacular space there stands the greatest of the mosque's three minarets, formidable and watchful like the bridge of a warship, from whose roofed deck the call to prayer sounds now as it has sounded down the centuries. Once, I suppose, incantations of the priests of Jupiter were heard here, and one of the mosque's minarets is based upon a tower of the pagan temple. Then there resounded hymns of Christian piety, and even now there remains preserved in its shrine within the prayer hall the alleged head of John the Baptist.

It is the unmistakable aura of Islam that today proclaims the sanctity of the Great Mosque of the Umayyads at Damascus, but I like to think that the place also expresses, in the ancient continuity of its history and the calm, kind splendour of its architecture, everything holiest in the beliefs of all the world.

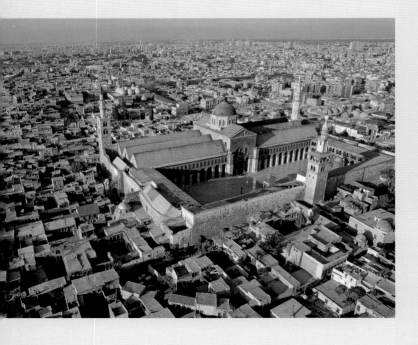

FAR LEFT: An aerial view of bustling Damascus, dominated by the courtyard and three minarets of the Umayyad Mosque.

LEFT: A detail of the mosaic on the main façade. Although many of the mosque's mosaics have been lost over time, the upper parts of nearly all of the walls would once have been decorated in this way, the lower parts being clad in marble. Most of the mosaics depict villages or isolated houses among stylized plants and trees and are thought to be visions of paradise.

ABOVE: Women sit in one of the courtyard archways, shading themselves from the Syrian heat.

RIGHT: The colonnaded quadrangle around which the mosque is built provides a meeting place for worshippers. The freestanding octagonal structure is the Dome of the Treasury, a receptacle once used for the safe storage of public funds.

Istanbul, Turkey

HAGIA SOPHIA

For 900 years, this mountainous hulk of a building was a Christian cathedral, then for 500 years a Muslim mosque. It has not only felt the tread of mighty emperors and sultans, but also suffered the cruel predations of invading armies. Indeed, for a place of worship, Hagia Sophia ("Holy Wisdom") bears more than its fair share of scars. Many of its once-glorious Byzantine mosaics have been either damaged or destroyed, while its sumptuous Islamic carpets have been rolled up and removed, following the building's conversion into a museum in 1935.

Today the two religions co-exist inside, locked in a state of suspended disharmony. Gigantic wooden discs, bearing the names of Allah and his prophet Muhammad, stare across at restored gold images of Christ Pantocrator ("All Powerful"). One faith (Islam) forbids the representation of the human or divine form, the other (Christianity) exults in it, and here the contradiction finds dramatic expression.

But while the works of art on the walls may give off conflicting messages, the building itself communicates an aura of might, with its sturdy stone columns, echoing marble floors and great slabs of stone from across the Mediterranean world (Egyptian porphyry, black stone from the Bosphorus, yellow from Syria). The great central dome soars 180 feet (55 metres) above the floor, pierced by 40 windows, through which stream shafts of light, giving the effect that it is floating, weightless, suspended by some heavenly force.

It took 10,000 labourers to build this immense structure, and by the time it was officially consecrated in 537CE, it was already the third Christian cathedral to have been built on this site (the first was in 360CE). Since then Hagia Sophia has endured the very worst that humankind (wars and looting) and nature (fires and earthquakes) can visit upon it. And it is still standing.

ABOVE: The Hagia Sophia exterior. The minarets were a later, Islamic addition.

RIGHT: The vast, echoing interior, which displays the evidence of both Christian and Muslim worship.

Semien Wollo Zone, Ethiopia

LALIBELA

BY PICO IYER

Ethiopia's rock-church New Jerusalem

Everywhere you look there are petitioners dressed all in white and priests with long, dark beards, burning-eyed, rocking back and forth over their leathery, hand-sized copies of the Bible. The hillsides around the rock churches are clogged with hooded, robed figures, hundreds of them. As the sun comes up, and the priests stand under rainbowed umbrellas, haloed by clouds of frankincense, pilgrims called Bethlehem and Solomon and Abraham follow along, having walked two weeks to be in this sacred space.

Nuns sit in lightless cells in two-storey huts, white crosses on their iron doors; boys play ox-skin drums and sistrums; the places here are called Golgotha and Nazareth and the Jordan, so that believers who cannot go to Jerusalem can find a New Jerusalem closer to home. "This is heaven," said a guide, as he led me one New Year's Day around the eleven 700-year-old churches carved entirely out of red rock. "As soon as you step here, you have set foot in heaven."

Much of Ethiopia is something like a pulsing, chanting church, sustaining the oldest Christian culture in the world, its shepherds and donkeys and olive trees reminding you of a tradition that has barely changed in sixteen centuries. This is where the original Garden of Eden stood, some say, and others believe that the Ark of the Covenant was buried here; certainly it was the home of the Queen of Sheba, and to this day it observes the Julian Calendar, with thirteen months in every year. The Book of Enoch (attributed to the great grandfather of Noah and son of Jared) exists only in the Ethiopian language of Ge'ez.

Yet all the intensity and power of Ethiopia, where prayer shakes the heart as in no place I've seen save Tibet, comes to a point in Lalibela, a remote cluster of places of worship reached by unpaved road (the car's wheels spinning in dry creekbeds). Light streams through the cross-shaped windows;

ABOVE: A priest stands at the entrance to the church of Bete Gabriel-Rufael, one of the eleven "rock churches" at Lalibela .

LEFT: The cross-shaped church of Bete Giyorgis. The structure is hewn entirely out of the rock, its roof sitting level with the ground.

swinging censers fill the ancient spaces with incense; boys dart among the underground passageways, while priests in purple robes, golden crosses in their hands, chant softly in the dim light.

A truly sacred place is not one where people have worshipped or where history was made: it is one that lives and breathes and sobs and chokes the heart. Lalibela, with its men clutching staffs, its gaunt-bearded deacons from the Book of Kings, its silences, is such a place. The Emperor came to pray here when the first of Mussolini's Blackshirts arrived, speaking for something classic against the majestic spaces of the high plateau.

For Ethiopians, the rock-cut churches were built with the help of angels, one of whom visited King Lalibela in the late 12th century and instructed him to build a city in the north. For historians, the structures, built at 7,500 feet (2,300 metres) above sea level, took 23 years to construct, using masons from Spain and Greece and even India. For the rest of us, the site is just a place to expand and deepen our sense of the possible. From 1544 to around 1868, the New Jerusalem was seen by not a single European. Now it is there for anyone who is prepared to make the long pilgrimage across the plains.

ABOVE: A priest reading in the dark interior of the Bete Golgotha Michael rock church in Lalibela.

LEFT: A priest rests in the window of another rock church.

Jerusalem, Israel

TEMPLE MOUNT

No other site on Earth can assert such a concentration of spiritual significance as a 35-acre man-made esplanade in Jerusalem's Old City: probably, nowhere else can assert such political and historical importance, either. In whatever terms it is viewed, and whatever the faith of the judge, an understanding of Temple Mount could be said to be critical to our conception of what it means to be human.

Within its boundaries, the vast compound hosts Judaism's holiest site, and Islam's third holiest. In the Torah, Jews are told that this is where Adam was created from dust. For Muslims, the golden curve of the Dome of the Rock marks Muhammad's destination when he journeyed to Jerusalem, and the site of his ascent to heaven. A short distance away, just beyond the compound's limits, the Church of the Holy Sepulchre stands on Golgotha, where Christ is said to have been crucified. And on the other side of the Western – or Wailing – Wall, Jews from Israel and around the world congregate at the holiest site at which they are able to pray, believed to be the only remnant of their Holy Temple, posting their missives to God in the cracks between the limestone slabs.

The Jews who pray at the Wailing Wall may not do so within the Temple Mount compound itself, for reasons both religious and political – on the one hand lest they stray, unclean, into the unknown location of the holiest spot in the world; on the other because of fears that the long-disputed claim to the site's spiritual sovereignty may once more spark violence. The nervous-looking policemen who patrol the site are just as much a part of its fabric now as the faithful. There is something strange about such dissonance in what remains, nonetheless, what it has long been: one of the most spiritually charged places on the planet.

ABOVE: Temple Mount and the Dome of the Rock. Sacred to Jews, Christians and Muslims alike, the site is visited by thousands of pilgrims every day.

RIGHT: The Dome of the Rock, constructed in the 7th century CE, is the oldest surviving Islamic building in the world.

Meroë, Sudan

MEROË PYRAMIDS

The pyramid tombs of Meroë rise from the desert like islands in an ocean of sand, mute witnesses to the glories of Nubia, an ancient African civilization that flourished until the Middle Ages. Meroë was one of the most important Nubian cities and, for nearly 700 years from ca. 300BCE, it was the capital of Kush, a Nubian kingdom. Little remains of the great Kushite city save hundreds of mounds of brick and stone, and the scant ruins of Egyptian-inspired palaces and temples. But Meroë was not just one city, but two. Alongside the city of the living stood a sacred city for the dead – 200 pyramid tombs, in which the monarchs and nobility were buried.

More than 40 dead sovereigns were mummified and sealed in the pyramids, which were considered entrances to the eternal afterlife. Laid to rest in underground chambers, these powerful rulers – male and female – were surrounded by rich objects imported from as far away as the Greek world. The Nubians admired Egyptian culture but the Kushite pyramids are no mere slavish copies. These homes for the dead are much smaller and steeper than those of Egypt, built in stepped courses rather than smooth-sided, and rising at most to around 100 feet (30 metres). From their peaks the souls of the departed would have risen to the gods.

You could be forgiven for assuming that many of the pyramids owe their crumbled state to time and the gritty, stinging desert winds that sandblast the site. In fact, an Italian adventurer systematically wrecked 40 of them in the 1830s in a quest for gold. A few of these have been restored.

Attached to the pyramids are chapels where the Kushites performed sacred funeral rites and offerings. Inside, beautifully incised friezes show the monarchs in profile, many protected by the wings of Isis. The worn inscriptions are in Meroitic script, which has never been translated. To this day, the dead of Meroë keep many of their secrets.

RIGHT: Some of the 200 pyramids in which the Kushites buried their dead, to help them on their journey to the afterlife.

near Bulawayo, Zimbabwe

MATOBO HILLS

BY ALEXANDER McCALL SMITH

Bewitching dwelling place of the spirits

The Matobo Hills – or the Matopos, as they used to be called – are one of the most spiritually significant sites in Africa. They are difficult to describe without resorting to language at the very edge of meaning: only the most delicate word-brush can capture the distilled beauty of this great expanse of granite hills. They cannot be described as towering; they are not all that high; they cannot be said to be forbidding, nor wild, nor desolate. They are peaceful, but not domestic or tamed. But what they are is utterly bewitching.

The hills stretch south from just outside the Zimbabwean city of Bulawayo. This was built on the site of the old capital of the kingdom of Matabeleland, established by the Ndebele king, Mizilikazi. Mizilikazi is buried in a cave on the periphery of the Matobo Hills and for many years this grave was largely unknown and unmarked. I remember, over twenty years ago, finding my way to the house of the spirit-medium who guarded it. She was, as I recall, an agreeable and well-mannered woman called Alice, who led me through thick bush to an opening in the rock. There she recited a long Ndebele praise-poem, of the sort traditionally incanted before Zulu and Ndebele kings. Peering into the cave, one could just make out the fragments of the king's old ox-wagon (the king's body had been placed in a separate part of the cave and walled in with stones). It was impossible not to be struck by the significance of this spot, the final resting place of the founder of a kingdom that was to be caught up in such a sad and disappointing subsequent history.

Further into the hills, nature piles granite boulder upon granite boulder in impossible mounds. These great boulders are grey-green with lichen; red in the evening sun; shimmering blue in the distance; and almost white in the early light of dawn. There is a stillness about them that seems to rise above and overcome the insistent shriek of cicadas; even in the rainy season, when the rain falls in thundering white curtains, the hills keep their quality of quietude.

For the Ndebele people, these hills are the dwelling place of ancestral spirits, whose influence may still be felt in the lives of their descendants. These beliefs have been overlaid by imported Christianity, but still have an attenuated role in the lives of many. Spirit and place are intimately linked, and this is particularly true of one of the most beautiful places in the Matobo, the great hill known as Malindidzimu, the "Dwelling Place of the Spirits". This is sacred ground to the Ndebele people, and was chosen by Cecil Rhodes to be the site of his grave. Modern visitors, even those who may be blissfully unaware of the full sorrow of this country's history, are invariably impressed into silence as they stand on this summit and look out over a vista of hills that seems to go on forever, and beyond, to some distant Africa of our longing.

RIGHT, ABOVE: Piles of granite boulders at the summit of Malindidzimu, the "Dwelling Place of the Spirits" in the Matobo Hills.

RIGHT: A view of the thickets and rocky outcrops of the lower Matobo Hills.

Bandiagara, Mali

DOGON SHRINES

Most of the Dogon people live in villages on the Bandiagara escarpment in central Mali, which rises above the surrounding plains for around 100 miles (160 km). For the Dogon, this dramatic landscape is sacred, and almost everywhere you go in Dogon country you will come across holy stones, pools and caves. The most sacred places of all are the remarkable shrines found at the heart of every Dogon village. Like the surrounding flat-roofed village houses, with their conical thatched granaries, these sanctuaries – principally Lebe and Binu shrines – are built mainly of mud and seem to emerge from the soil like natural features of the landscape.

Lebe shrines contain the altar of the earth god Lebe, the most important of the Dogon deities. The first being to die,

Lebe was resurrected as a snake, setting in motion the whole cycle of birth, death and regrowth. At the Lebe shrine the village chief, the Hogon, conducts rituals to encourage the fruitfulness of the land. According to ancient Dogon creation stories, Lebe was one of four pairs of twins, or Nommos, who descended to Earth from a "cosmic egg" in the stars at the beginning of creation. They became the ancestors of humankind, and their spirits are said to reside in the eight niches on the façade of a typical Lebe shrine.

The second type of shrine is dedicated to the Dogon cult of supernatural protector beings known as Binu. These sanctuaries are often adorned with symbolic paintings and reliefs in the traditional Dogon colours of black, white and red, as well as a range of earthen hues. A striking feature

of the shrines is the curious white streaks on the façades – offerings of millet porridge poured onto the walls during rituals to ask the Binu spirits for rain and an abundant harvest. On some shrines the four or eight turrets are crowned with ostrich eggs, symbols of fertility and the cosmic egg, as at the Great Mosque of Djenné (*see pp104–5*).

Here again is the intimate relationship between earth, animals and people that forms a sacred thread binding together all aspects of Dogon life.

BELOW: Traditional Dogon symbolic paintings in the Songo village of Bandiagara. This spot is the site of a circumcision ceremony that takes place every three years. These paintings are similar in style to those found on some Binu shrines.

BELOW, LEFT: A Dogon shrine dedicated to the Binu – supernatural protector beings. The shrine's turrets are crowned with ostrich eggs, symbolizing purity and fertility.

FOLLOWING PAGES: An abandoned Dogon village built into the cliff face.

Saudi Arabia

MECCA

A bustling, cosmopolitan city of nearly two million inhabitants, complete with multi-lane highways, shops, apartment blocks, offices and hotels, Mecca, or *Makkah*, creates at first sight the impression of modern, urban normality. But this impression is deceptive, because Mecca is like no other city on Earth. It is the birthplace of Islam, and those of other faiths may not enter its limits, which include the city itself and several other sites in the arid valley that surrounds it. At Mecca's heart stands the great Haram Mosque, site of the ancient Ka'ba shrine, a rectangular building containing the sacred Black Stone, possibly a meteorite. For one billion Muslims this spot is the holiest place in the world.

One sacred duty of all Muslims is to pray five times daily in the direction of Mecca. Another is to undertake the *Hajj*, the pilgrimage to Mecca, at least once in their lifetime, if they are able to. Mecca is inseparable from the Hajj. The event takes place in Dhul-Hijjah, the twelfth month of the Islamic lunar calendar, when millions of Muslims descend from all over the world. Hence the city's many hotels – they are not for tourists, but for pilgrims.

The Hajj is a great act of spiritual renewal. It is arduous, and involves visiting not only the Ka'ba but several other sacred sites in the valley over the course of several days. It begins just outside the city at the *Miqat*, or "Entry", where pilgrims ritually bathe, don special seamless white robes,

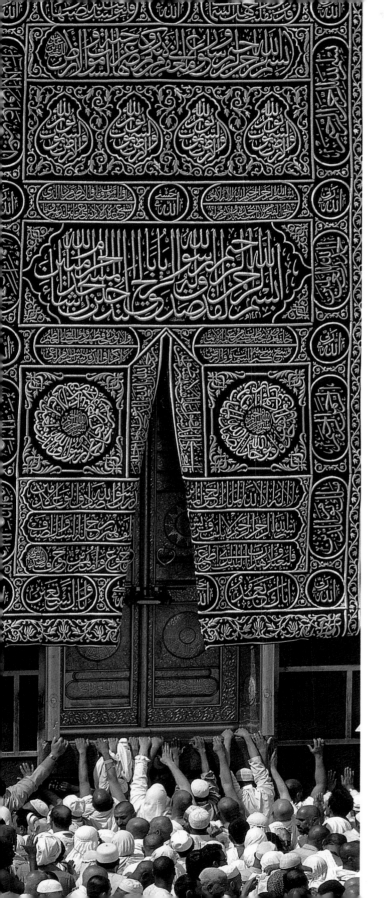

pray to Allah and dedicate themselves to the Hajj. They then go to the Haram Mosque for Tawaf, the ritual of walking seven times around the Ka'ba, which stands in the mosque's vast asymmetrical, colonnaded courtyard.

But that is just the beginning – the *Umra*, or "Lesser Hajj". To fulfil their sacred duty, over the coming days pilgrims will walk seven times back and forth between Mecca's sacred hills of Safa and Marwa, stand in the open praising Allah in the blistering heat of the Valley of Arafat, visit the Plain of Mina to throw pebbles at three stone pillars that symbolize Satan, sleep under the stars on the Plain of Muzdalifah, and perform a ritual sacrifice. After another Tawaf in the Haram they return to Mina, and then, finally, go back into the city for one last circumambulation of the Ka'ba.

With this, the Hajj is complete, and the pilgrims return to their homelands and their normal lives – but spiritually cleansed, at one with Allah, and entitled to be known as *Hajji* or, if they are women, *Hajja*: "Pilgrim". There is a saying that a pilgrim may leave Mecca – but Mecca never leaves the pilgrim.

LEFT: Pilgrims reach to touch and kiss the Black Stone and the door of the Ka'ba, Islam's most sacred sanctuary and pilgrimage shrine.

FAR LEFT: Worshippers surround the Ka'ba in the courtyard of the Haram Mosque, Mecca. At the start and finish of the Hajj (pilgrimage to Mecca), pilgrims must circle the Ka'ba seven times.

Ararat Marz, Armenia
KHOR VIRAP MONASTERY

Khor Virap Monastery is a small, unadorned church and chapel set in a wide, flat plain in front of the holy peak of Mount Ararat – where the Bible says Noah's ark came to rest after the flood. This seemingly humble monastery's significance owes less to its dramatic setting than it does to the story of Armenia's conversion to become the first Christian country in the world.

The monastery itself, which consists of a church, smaller chapel and the monks' cells and refectory, is set within fortress-like walls. The 17th-century church, St Astvatsatsin, is built of red brick and has scarcely any ornament, except for a few carvings of the Armenian cross, or even windows, on its exterior. Inside, the basilica is equally austere, a small painted altarpiece providing almost the only decoration.

Khor Virap is Armenian for "deep pit", and concealed underneath the nearby St Gevorg Chapel, built in the 7th century, there is a tunnel cut into the rock of the floor. Metal rungs set in the stone lead to a cramped, blackened stone dungeon, 20 feet (6 metres) underground, whose gloom is penetrated only by a shaft of sunlight from the tiny window hole and a few candles competing for limited air.

This claustrophobic pit is where the patron saint of Armenia, Gregory the Illuminator, was held for thirteen years in the 3rd century CE, incarcerated by King Trdat III. According to legend, the king later developed a disease that turned him into a wild boar. After Gregory was released he was able to cure the king and then converted him, and therefore Armenia as a whole, to Christianity.

RIGHT: Khor Virap Monastery, with Mount Ararat in the background. Located on top of one of the only hills in the Ararat valley, the monastery is among the most popular pilgrimage sites in Armenia.

Arabah, Jordan

PETRA

BY PICO IYER

A city hidden in the desert

You walk in through a tiny cleft in the sandstone rocks, and walk and walk through what feels like a narrowing gorge, so thin at points it is barely 4 yards wide, so high you cannot see the sky. You keep walking, for fifteen minutes or more, through a red-rock gorge so lightless and silent you might be slipping along the bottom of the Grand Canyon. Then, suddenly, you step out into the light and there, before you, 135 feet (40 metres) tall and 90 feet (27 metres) wide, is a vast, six-columned palace, carved out of sheer rock, with classical figures all around it: the "Treasury".

A little further on, you make your way through a slightly wider passageway and pass the "Street of Façades", with tombs in every corner. Then you step out again into the light and face a huge open space that resembles a city hidden in a desert. Here is an amphitheatre where originally 3,000 spectators could assemble. Five hundred tombs sit in and among the slopes and caves. In the distance is another structure (the "Monastery"), even larger than the Treasury.

The "red-rock city" of Petra was first created by the Nabataeans, within the Shara mountains of southern Jordan, in the five centuries before the birth of Christ. The area had already been inhabited for more than 6,000 years – some of the earliest farmers in history had settled among these hills and wadis – and the Nabataeans, a nomadic tribe from western Arabia, realized that the secret location (Rakeem, as they called it) could make a perfect home. From here they could control trading routes leading in all four directions, to Gaza, to Damascus, to Aqaba and across the desert. In its heyday – during Jesus' lifetime – Petra was home to 30,000 people and its enterprising residents devised their own script (a precursor to Arabic) and built their own ingenious waterways and dams.

ABOVE: The entrance of one of the 500 tombs carved into the Petra sandstone.

LEFT: The elaborate palace known as Al Khasneh or the "Treasury" glimpsed through the gorge that approaches it.

When the Romans took over Petra in 106ce, they, too, saw how valuable a hidden city could be, and added baths and colonnades, so that Petra (the Greek word for "rock") became a new kind of capital, larger even than before. Then history moved on and the whole city fell into silence again, concealed behind its towering walls of rock. For more than 500 years, almost nobody knew the place existed. The Bedouins who lived in the region took pains to preserve its secrecy. Only in 1812, when the Swiss explorer Johann Ludwig Burckhardt stepped into the site, drawn by stories of a lost city in the mountains, did Europe learn of this hidden treasure.

You can feel in Petra today all those centuries of seclusion and untouchedness. The city sits like a ship in a bottle sent to us from a civilization of which we know little. Part of its charm for the modern visitor is that it bustles with tea-stalls, camel-bells and goatherds, and children playing tag among the rock-hewn cliffs and wildflowers. You can climb up to the "High Place of Sacrifice" and enjoy a picnic near where Bedouins used to camp in goat-skin tents. At night, sometimes, the site is open for performances of classical Arabic music, lit by small lanterns in front of the Treasury.

Yet the power of the site – what lifts the spirit and expands the senses – is the feeling of tiptoeing into a wonder undiscovered. I chanced to visit Petra at dawn on the first day of the new millennium. I walked for twenty minutes or so through the shadowy defiles, and then I stepped out to see only one other figure – a lone Japanese tourist – in the great expanse. A little later, in 2003, a whole new complex was found beneath the Treasury, as if to remind us that Petra has more secrets than it's ever given up. By most counts, 95 per cent of the ancient city still awaits discovery, standing for a world we're only just beginning to discern.

RIGHT: The dramatic "Urn Tomb" built high up the mountainside and accessible by climbing several flights of stairs.

Mashhad, Iran

SHRINE OF IMAM REZA

The Shrine of Imam Reza lies like an opulent jewel at the heart of the Haram-e-Razavi, a network of Islamic holy precincts in Mashhad. Eggshell blue domes, golden minarets and courtyard fountains recreate the garden of paradise. As the shadows lengthen and dusk falls, the *adhan*, the Muslim call to worship, pours into the evening air, proclaiming the greatness of God. A respectful crowd make their way to prayer. Some bareheaded women pause to cover themselves with delicately patterned *chadors* before entering.

For Shi'ite Muslims the first twelve Imams were infallible – perfect human beings who offered a spiritual example for others. Imam Reza was regarded as a man of unusual scholarship and remarkable integrity. After being elected caliph he was poisoned by a jealous competitor in 818CE. This site of his tomb has been a sacred destination for pilgrims for more than a thousand years.

Seven courtyards are linked to the inner areas of the mosque by external hallways referred to as *bast*, meaning "sanctuaries". These lead to 21 internal halls surrounding the burial chamber. Tiny tiles glazed gold and silver decorate the halls, catching the light of the chandeliers overhead and throwing it back from a hundred different directions.

Toward the centre of the shrine the geometric patterns on the walls become ever more intricate. The mosaic tiles reveal patterns within patterns, culminating in the splendour of the central chamber with its gold filigree, fretwork and

fine marble. The outside of the dome over the tomb is covered in sheets of gold. Directly under the dome is the *zarih*, a gilt latticed cage shrouding Imam Reza's tomb. Reaching the *zarih* is the high point of this Islamic pilgrimage, and worshippers throng round touching and kissing the covering to show their respect for the eighth of the twelve Imams of Shi'ite Islam.

BELOW: Originally built in the 9th century, and reconstructed several times since, the Shrine of Imam Reza houses the remains of the eighth Imam of Shi'ite Islam. As many as 20 million pilgrims visit the site each year.

LEFT, BELOW: The opulent domes and minarets of the shrine. The golden dome covers Imam Reza's mausoleum, containing the gilt *zarih* that encloses his tomb.

Makadikadi, Botswana

MAKADIKADI SALT PANS

BY ALEXANDER McCALL SMITH

Pristine plain of precious emptiness

Most of the sites that we consider to be spiritual are associated in some way with ourselves, with people, with what we have done. The famous Bodhi tree in Bodh Gaya (*see pp172–3*) was an important tree for Buddhists not because it was a tree, but because it was the tree under which Buddha received enlightenment. Places may be of significance for Christians because in those places saints had visions, or did great works, or because some relic of that saint is preserved there. All of that is understandable: spirituality is about the human spirit and we may need physical reminders of what that spirit has achieved, or indeed suffered, in the past.

But what about places where there is nobody – or very few people – and where we nonetheless react in a spiritual way to unmediated natural beauty? There are such places, and I think that our reaction to them may be deeply spiritual. Although they do not invoke man, they may lead to a sense of spiritual engagement with the earth itself, our home, the rock upon which we shall ultimately all be laid down.

Every country will have some little spot at least where the works of man are not to be seen and where we may look out upon a world that has nothing to do with man and his often corrupting presence. In Botswana, there are many pristine landscapes, where there are very few, if any, people. The Central Kalahari, for instance, is one such – a vast semi-desert whose only inhabitants are small bands of San, those remarkably adept people who still preserve, in some measure, hunter-gatherer skills. In the Makadikadi Pans, a great plain that stretches across hundreds of square miles, there seems to be nothing apart from sky and white salt earth, fringed by palm trees and thin savannah.

Why is it such a spiritual experience to stand beneath that sky? Emptiness. In many spiritual traditions there is talk of the cultivation of emptiness, or ridding the soul of distraction and the accreted complications of life. Make yourself empty. Put self and its concerns aside. That is difficult to do when everywhere about us we see frenzied human activity. But here in these empty places of Africa, we are by ourselves, in the world as it was created before we covered it with machines and concrete.

And at night, in the absence of light from human doings, the sky here can be almost white with constellation upon constellation of stars. I always look for the Southern Cross, hanging low in the sky; beyond the empty land, the empty southern seas; how small I am, how small we all are; how tiny our concerns and worries; how wide and wonderful the world.

LEFT AND FOLLOWING PAGES:
The vast, unpeopled expanse of the Makadikadi Salt Pans. This salt-crusted land was left behind after the lakes that were once here evaporated.

Marrakesh, Morocco

BEN YOUSSEF MADRASA

Founded in the 14th century, the Ben Youssef *madrasa*, or Islamic religious school, was remodelled in the 1560s by the Sa'adian sultans. The result was the largest *madrasa* (or *medersa* in Moroccan Arabic) west of Egypt. It is also one of the most beautiful, its reconstruction coinciding with the zenith of Moroccan architecture.

At its heart is a large arcaded courtyard, its serenity enhanced by the waters of a long rectangular ritual ablution pool in the centre. In these hushed environs, up until the 1960s, learned theologians (sheikhs) gave instruction in the Quran and Islamic theology to scholars from many Islamic lands. Off the courtyard is the hall where scholars prayed and the simple cells where they lived. It is a peaceful setting, a place for worship and contemplation amid the jostle of the city that can be glimpsed from some of the cells.

Throughout the *madrasa*, elaborate ornament on almost every wall, doorway, arch and pillar declaims the infinite glory, wisdom and mercy of Allah in geometric and floral motifs, alongside Quranic passages in stylized calligraphy. Chief among these is a phrase known as the *Bismallah*: "In the name of God the Merciful, the Compassionate". The mosaic tiling (*zellij*) around the lower part of the central courtyard displays all these elements in a rich palate of greens, blues and ochres.

Prominent among the motifs is the eight-pointed star, and the number eight is present again in the octagonal dome of the prayer hall. Eight has celestial significance in Islam: there are eight regions of paradise and eight angels hold up the throne of Allah on Judgment Day. Like the *madrasa* itself, such motifs serve two simple but elevated purposes: the glorification of God, and the spiritual enrichment of the beholder.

Isfahan, Iran

SHEIKH LOTFOLLAH MOSQUE

Sheikh Lotfollah Mosque (built in the early 17th century) is situated on the eastern flank of one of the most perfectly proportioned urban spaces in the world: Isfahan's ancient Naqsh-e Jahan (now Imam Khomeini) Square, an elegantly arcaded rectangle from which rise, at various points, some of the most glorious buildings in Iran. In contrast to the turquoise domes of its neighbouring mosques, Sheikh Lotfollah offers up a vast, smooth, radiant, pink-tiled bulb to the sun. At ground level, its faïence-tiled portals are covered in intricate blue, yellow and white stalactite work, a veritable ceramic honeycomb. But it is inside that the true wonders await.

Unlike other mosques, the Sheikh Lotfollah has no entrance courtyard, or minarets from which the _muezzin_ might summon the faithful – the reason being that this was a private place of worship, built especially for the man whose name it bears: a great Lebanese Islamic scholar (and son-in-law to the Safavid king Shah Abbas).

The approach, through a darkened entrance passage, does little to prepare you for the breathtaking power of the prayer hall within. The ceramic walls are not just covered in calligraphy, they are alive with it, Arabic script entwined like flower tendrils with arabesques and intricate floral designs. At first sight, the effect of the ceiling dome mosaic is like an enormous firework exploding above, the moment frozen in time at the point of brightest starburst. As your eyes adjust to the light, the image becomes that of a gigantic peacock's tail, the glory of its extended plumage enhanced by the sunlight that pours through the windows that pierce its base and a small hole in the ceiling. For the earthbound mortal, this is a glimpse of the divine.

New Delhi, India

JAMA MASJID

BY MARK TULLY

A thousand bowed heads, praying to an omnipotent God

ABOVE AND FOLLOWING PAGES: Crowds of devotees gather to pray outside the Jama Masjid at the festival of Eid al-Fitr, which marks the end of Ramadan.

RIGHT: Morning prayers in the mosque's prayer hall.

By setting Delhi's Jama Masjid, or "Friday mosque", on a hillock 35 feet (10 metres) high, the 17th-century Mughal Emperor Shah Jahan clearly intended that it should dominate the capital he built. The building is still an imposing presence in the area of the Indian capital now commonly known as old Delhi. The tall fluted minarets, the white marble domes of the prayer hall and the vast courtyard where the faithful in their thousands assemble for prayers symbolized the spiritual underpinning of Mughal rule, while the temporal power of the Emperor was represented by the sprawling Red Fort that was built nearby.

Every Friday thousands of Muslim men and boys wearing their white prayer caps scramble up the steps of the mosque and pour through the gates into the courtyard. Vast though the courtyard is, it can't contain all those who come to say their prayers on major festivals such as Eid al-Fitr, so the congregation spills into the narrow streets surrounding the mosque. The words of the sermon preached from the *mimbar* or pulpit, which was carved from one solid block of marble, are relayed by loudspeakers and can be heard far beyond the mosque's confines.

For me the sight of thousands of Muslims saying their Eid prayers in Delhi's Jama Masjid symbolizes India's commitment to uphold the freedom of citizens to practise their faith whatever it may be and to worship openly. This commitment is based on a tradition that goes back thousands of years, a tradition that accepts there are many ways to God and, therefore, there will be many ways to *worship* God. It's this tradition that has allowed almost all of the world's great religions to put down roots in India. So many different Hindu denominations have evolved through the centuries that many wonder whether Hinduism can even be called one religion. Christians believe their faith was first established in

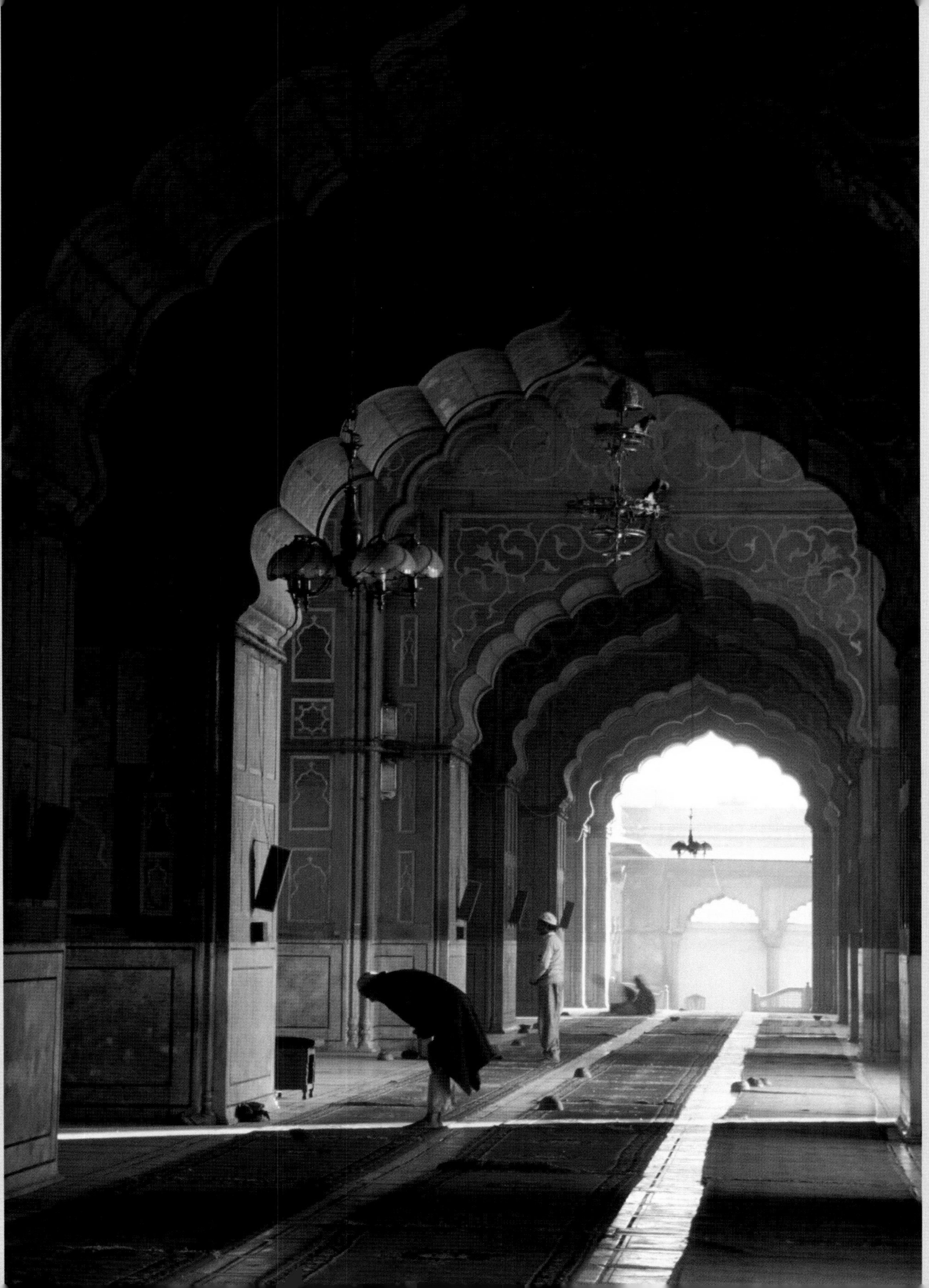

India by St Thomas, the doubting apostle. Muslims know that it was Arab traders who originally brought their faith to India in the early days of Islam.

When I watch the worshippers in the Jama Masjid, drawn up in lines as orderly as any military parade, thousands of heads bowing to the ground as one in acknowledgment of God's omnipotence, I am struck by the power of ritual to convey that omnipotence. For me it's the all-powerful God, the God shrouded in mystery, the God who is beyond reason who is being worshipped.

The prayers are in Arabic, the universal language of Islam. Every day millions and millions of Muslims around the world worship in the same language, and, wherever they are, all face the holy city of Mecca, the cradle of their faith. So for me the worshippers in the Jama Masjid are acknowledging a universal rather than a personal God, a God we should be in awe of, rather than a God who is our friend. In contrast to today's individualism, which lays such stress on spirituality and our personal experience of God, the Muslims praying in the Jama Masjid are members of the worldwide Islamic community. I believe that spirituality can so easily make God too small. The mystery of faith is that God is so small that he pays attention to each one of us and yet so vast that his power and presence are universal. As each individual says his personal prayers in Delhi's Jama Masjid, he is at the same time made aware of the grandeur of God.

Paro, Bhutan

TAKTSANG MONASTERY

ABOVE: A painted Buddha at Taktsang Monastery.

LEFT: The monastery buildings cling to the cliff-face over the Paro valley. They were built at the spot where Guru Rinpoche is supposed to have spent three months in meditation in the 8th century.

Known as the "Tiger's Nest" of Bhutan, the Taktsang Monastery perches nearly 10,000 feet (3,000 metres) above sea level, on the edge of a precipice in the foothills of the Himalayas. Simple, white-painted walls support the traditional flat roofs and delicately carved windows of this 16th-century Buddhist monastery, built at the spot where Buddhism is thought to have first emerged in Bhutan.

According to legend, in the 8th century the Guru Rinpoche or Padmasambhava, named as the second Buddha and credited with spreading Buddhism across Bhutan and Tibet, landed here on the back of a flying tigress. For three months the Guru meditated in a cave. He was believed to have miraculous powers, and the tigress was in fact his consort, Yeshe Tsogyal, whom he had transformed (hence the name Taktsang, "Tiger's Nest"). In 1692, almost one thousand years later, the monastery was built at this site to commemorate his visit.

High on a lonely mountain trail, Taktsang can only be approached by a two-hour hike or mule-ride. The monastery is often shrouded in mist, and the pilgrim may not even get a glimpse of his destination until he turns the last bend of the steeply winding path. The route climbs through the valley in a series of roughly hewn stone staircases, finally crossing a bridge in front of a waterfall before making its last steep ascent. Multicoloured strings of fluttering prayer flags stretch across the cliff faces and the intermittent sound of a bell tolls through the quiet valley. The monks may bestow a blessing on the traveller before he or she descends back into the mist.

After it was built, Taktsang remained unchanged in its tranquil cloudscape for more than 300 years. But in 1998 the monastery was burned almost to the ground by a fire. The structure took the best part of seven years to rebuild, using old drawings and photographs for reference, and the new building, paid for by the Bhutan government, is a triumph of this painstaking restoration.

Ayutthaya Province, Thailand

AYUTTHAYA

Ayutthaya was the capital of the Thai kingdom from 1351 until its destruction in 1767, during a devastating string of wars with the Burmese. It was founded by King Ramathibodi I (1314–69) and named for the ancient Indian city of Ayodhya, birthplace of the Hindu god Rama, of whom the king was believed to be a reincarnation. However, Ayutthaya became the royal seat at a time when Thai monarchs were establishing Buddhism as the state religion, and much of what can be seen at Ayutthaya today is the remains of a Buddhist city.

As you walk through the vast site of Ayutthaya – at its zenith in the 1600s it had a population of one million – ominous black scorchmarks are reminders of the terrible firestorm that engulfed the city during the sack of 1767. Nothing of the royal palaces, houses and other wooden buildings survived, but many stone temples and monasteries retain their grandeur, their damaged Buddhist statues and reliefs bearing witness to the beauty of the city at its height. An impression of the city's lost wooden buildings can

even be gleaned from stone balustrades delicately carved to imitate turned wood. The tantalizing fragments of stuccoed brick friezes show Khmer influences, but uniquely Thai styles evolved here, too, with many Buddhist reliquary towers or stupas (*chedi*) displaying the typical Thai "bell" or "lotus-bud" profile.

One of Ayutthaya's most stunning sacred complexes is the temple of Wat Chai Wattanaram, founded in 1629 by the tyrant King Prasat Tong as a memorial to his mother and also

BELOW, LEFT: The Wat Chai Wattanaram complex in Ayutthaya, constructed by King Prasat Tong in the 17th century. Its name means "Temple of long reign and glorious era".

BELOW: A meditating Buddha statue outside the temple complex.

as a statement of power. The complex is a stylized imitation of the universe, with a soaring central tower (*prang*) in the corncob-shaped Khmer style representing the mystic Mount Meru, the centre of the cosmos (*see p165*). Smaller *prang*s at the corners of the temple stand above chapels where serene meditating Buddhas sit in stark and poignant contrast to their fire-blackened surroundings.

ABOVE: A Buddha head emerging from the roots of a bodhi tree at Wat Phra Mahathat, one of the oldest temples in Ayutthaya.

LEFT: A monk prays by a Giant Reclining Buddha, the main shrine at Wat Lokaya Sutha.

Rajasthan, India
RANAKPUR TEMPLE

Deep in the Aravali hills, between Udaipur and Jodhpur, stands the beautiful 5th-century Jain temple of Ranakpur. Carved entirely out of white marble and surrounded by lush forest, the temple surveys its surroundings in each of the cardinal directions from its *chaumukha,* or "four faces". Fortress-solid, great slabs of stone rise out of the ground to support the bulk of the temple's lavish exterior, a grandiose edifice of cupolas, domes and turrets of soft grey marble.

Inside, 1,444 intricately carved pillars support the roof, each one unique in its design. Soft light filters through the marble, changing its colour from grey to gold, as the sun moves across the sky. Only the saffron and red fabrics of robes brighten the surroundings as the monks and pilgrims pass between the pillars, through pools of light into shadow.

In the 5th century a Jain businessman named Dharna Sah had a vision that he should build a magnificent temple in honour of Adinath, the first *Tirthankara* (enlightened being) and founder of Jainism, also known as Rishabhadeva. He approached the local monarch, Rana Kumbha, to ask him for land on which to build. The king obliged him, and the temple was named "Ranakpur" in gratitude for his munificence.

The result is one of the most harmonious religious buildings in India. The temple is still in constant use and visitors are welcome, although, according to the Jainist principle of *ahimsa* (non-violence to all things), they are asked not to bring any leather into the temple, including shoes. As you walk through Ranakpur, past delicate marble carvings and solemnly praying monks, the loving craftsmanship of so many individual souls is striking, and the atmosphere of devotion utterly absorbing.

RIGHT: A few of the 1,444 uniquely carved marble pillars at the Ranakpur Temple. The temple was built in the 5th century by businessman Dharna Sah, after he experienced a divine vision.

Kyoto, Japan

RYOANJI ZEN DRY GARDEN

BY PICO IYER

A riddle in rock and sand

The fifteen stones set in a compact ocean of raked sand stand for the islands of Japan, adrift on the ocean of time. No, they represent a tigress crossing a river with her cubs. Far from it: they show mountain peaks rising above the clouds. It is the nature of places of the spirit to present questions more than they do answers: they offer us a mirror and in them what we see, quite often, is just a reflection of who we are. Part of the special power of the most famous rock garden in the world, at Ryoanji, is that from no point, it is traditionally said, can you see all fifteen stones. Some truth, or mystery, is always beyond your grasp.

When you visit Kyoto, the capital of Japan for more than 1,000 years (from 794 to 1868), you learn that there are more than 1,600 temples, 400 shrines and three imperial villas around the hills that ring it on three sides and tucked in among the thin lanes and wooden houses that persist downtown. There are seventeen World Heritage sites, and rock gardens, strolling gardens, palace gardens, even a moss garden with 130 different kinds of moss. Golden pavilions stand above ponds, the floors of an old castle mimic the sound of a nightingale, Zen temples and bright Shinto shrines and tombs and little folkloric talismans haunt every narrow backstreet, turning the whole city into a shrine of Japaneseness.

But for most visitors, the centre of all these meditative treasures is in the northwest, in the simple, opaque, abstract arrangement of fifteen boulders at Ryoanji (the name means "Temple of the Peaceful Dragon"). They were first placed there in the late 15th century, perhaps by the great Zen-inflected artist Soami, and are regarded as the high point of the *karesansui*, or "dry landscape" school of garden design. The Zen temple,

belonging to the Rinzai school, was once a family estate of the ruling Fujiwara family, and contains seven imperial tombs, and a small stone basin, whose inscription reads "What you have is all you need." You sit on a long, elevated wooden veranda in front of the Abbot's residence and look at the gravel before you – no water, no trees, nothing but moss on the rocks on the raked gravel, 75 by 29 feet (23 by 9 metres) wide – and you start to see what is not there as much as what tangibly is.

The last time I visited Ryoanji – I've lived in Kyoto for more than 22 years now – I noticed, really for the first time, that there are beautiful parks and extravagant gardens around the temple grounds, leaves turning a brilliant red and gold and yellow under the sharpened blue skies of November. There is a teahouse, a lake, an inscription above the gate saying "Cloud Garden" and behind the low walls that surround the raked garden on three sides you can see cherry trees, cedars and pines.

But still my mind, and my feet, keep coming back to this ageless, irregular arrangement of grey stones, slipped into the place like a secret note inside a package. Maybe they represent the character for "heart" or "mind". Maybe they speak for what the mind – or heart – does with what it cannot understand. And maybe they just serve as a training in attention, and a reminder that what you have is really all you need.

LEFT, ABOVE: Gardens and pathway at the entrance to Ryoanji.

LEFT AND FOLLOWING PAGES: The Ryoanji dry garden was created in the 15th century. Fifteen rocks rest on a large rectangle of gravel, which is raked around them daily.

Adam's Peak, Sri Lanka

HOLY FOOTPRINT

Adam's Peak rises majestically from a skirt of deep-green forest in Sri Lanka's central highlands. Its bare stone upper reaches form a natural pyramid that is all the more awe-inspiring for the lack of any comparable heights nearby. Even from a distance it is easy for any of the thousands of pilgrims who flock here each year to sense the numinous presence that has long made this the island's holiest site.

The relic that serves as the focus of attention is a mark on a boulder on the mountain's flat summit. Measuring 5¼ by 2½ feet (1.6 by 0.75 metres), the print is held sacred by the followers of all the region's main religions. For Sri Lanka's majority Buddhists this is the footprint of the Buddha himself; Hindu Tamils believe it was left by the god Shiva; while Christians associate it with St Thomas, and Muslims with Adam, the first man. The print is now housed inside a small shrine.

The footprint may have helped to seal the peak's reputation as a holy site, but for most of the multitude who come here the true attraction is the mountain itself. They make their way up the 2-mile (3-km) track to the summit in the small hours of the night, guided by electric lights installed after World War II. At the top they wait expectantly in the predawn darkness, straining to catch a glimpse of the sun rising over the horizon before drinking in the spectacle of the first light spreading over the eastern sky. Then they hurry across to the other side of the summit to see another wonder: the extraordinary, triangular shadow that the peak casts over the misty hills to the west, as geometrically regular as if it had been drawn by some divine mathematician's hand.

RIGHT: Adam's Peak with Maskeliya Lake in the foreground. Thousands of pilgrims scale this mountain each year to watch the sun rise and catch a glimpse of the Holy Footprint - believed to have been left behind by the Buddha, Shiva, St Thomas or Adam, by Buddhists, Hindus, Christians and Muslims respectively.

Rangoon, Myanmar

SHWEDAGON PAGODA

Shwedagon sits like some great, golden spaceship, overlooking the inner parklands of Rangoon – the main city of Myanmar (or Burma). Pilgrims ascend via steep, stone stairs, flanked at the entrance by the figures of two giant *chinthe*, or mythical lions. The way up is shaded, and thronged on either side by stall vendors selling incense sticks, prayer flags and statuettes of the Buddha.

Once at the top, the visitor is blinded by the brilliant glare of reflected sunlight from the 326 feet (100 metre) high stupa, covered on its lower extremities by gold leaf, and on its upper reaches by 13,153 solid gold plates. Enshrined at the Pagoda's topmost point gleams a 276-carat diamond.

The reason the site is held in such veneration is the presence of sacred Buddhist relics. Although the existing structure was only erected in 1769, following an earthquake, legend tells that the original stupa was built 2,500 years ago by two merchant brothers. Entrusted by the Buddha with eight of his hairs, the brothers were instructed to enshrine them in Burma. It is said that when they deposited the hairs, gems rained down from heaven like hailstones, and the trees in the Himalayas bore fruit out of season.

Today, as for centuries past, bare-foot worshippers walk clockwise around the scorching-hot marble terraces, passing through forests of smaller golden pagodas and pausing for an astrological reading at the planetary shrine that corresponds to the day on which they were born. The whole scene is played out to the ceaseless accompaniment of prayer bells, from the small and tinkling to the weighty and booming. Only at night does this sound cease.

Sitting proudly on its hilltop throne, the Shwedagon continues to be not just an enduring spiritual symbol, but a potent political rallying point for the Burmese people.

Gangdisê Mountains, Tibet

MOUNT KAILASH

This pyramidal Himalayan giant, standing 21,778 feet (6,638 metres) high, is held in reverence by the followers of four separate religions: Buddhists, Hindus, Jains and adherents of Tibet's indigenous Bön faith. Located in the extreme southwest of the country, near the border with India, its slopes remain off limits to climbers, and mountaineers now consider this the world's most significant unconquered peak.

The mountain's religious associations are many and varied. Hindus believe that a mythologized version of the mountain, Mount Meru, is the spiritual centre of the universe: the god Shiva and his consort Parvati are said to sit in meditation on its summit. Tibetans link it with Guru Rinpoche, who helped establish Buddhism as the nation's principal faith in the 8th century CE (*see p151*). According to a legend of the Bön tradition, this was the scene of a famous spiritual contest between their champion Naro Bon-chong and the Buddhist holy man Milarepa. Jains believe that their founder, Rishabhadeva, attained nirvana on its flanks.

Believers in all four religions continue to make regular pilgrimages to the mountain's foot, following a trail 32 miles (50 km) long that circles its base. (Mounting the slopes themselves is considered an act of impiety that can result in bad karma or even death.) Traditionally, Hindus and Buddhists move in a clockwise direction around the path, while supporters of the Bön and Jain faiths take the opposite tack. Some pilgrims choose to practise prostration all along the route, moving forward a body-length at a time, an ordeal that takes at least four weeks.

Hatsukaichi, Japan

MIYAJIMA ISLAND BY ANDREW MOTION

A complex address to the spirit

Ten minutes out from Hiroshima harbour, peering back from the ferry at the skull-dome that remembers the epicentre of the blast, then forward into the sunlight, I watch Itsukushima Island rise like the backdrop in a woodcut, then harden and become the whole picture. Miyajima Island, to give it the popular name. The Shrine Island: mountainous (with a thick pelt of forest), tiny (12 square miles), and sparsely populated (2,000 people, not counting the tourists). The ferry carves its signature alongside the jetty, then completes it with a flourish. I have arrived in a parallel world, one which changes with every new arrival browsing for trinkets in the tourist-lanes, but which nevertheless stays as it was in the beginning – the trees and plants deliberately untended, the shrine adored but imperturbable.

This shrine was originally established in the time of the Empress Suiko, then given its present form by the warrior-courtier Taira no Kiyomori; in 1555 a further large building, the Senjo-kaku, was settled on a hill overlooking everything. As I stoop into the orange-painted labyrinth of the temple-complex, I am immediately concentrated, focussed by the twin spirits of ingenuity and naturalness. There is no metal anywhere, not even nails, and the slatted wooden floors have been worn smooth by the tread of generations. In the elaborate and dark cave-altars, hand-written messages shimmer in the sea-breeze. At the end of it all, also concentrated by the low ceilings and tight angles, a view opens towards the silver page of the ocean, interrupted by the riveting punctuation mark of the *torii*.

The *torii* is the gateway, and I should have visited there first. But I am the wrong way round by design, not accident. By the time I emerge from the temple-walks, the tide has turned, the ocean has withdrawn, and the pebbly, whispering

ABOVE: Priests walking across one of the pathways in the temple-complex of the Itsukushima Shrine.

LEFT, ABOVE: Looking over the pagodas of Miyajima Island towards the famous *torii* gate and the sea beyond.

LEFT: A footbridge surrounded by autumnal Japanese maple trees at Momijidani Park, Miyajima.

ground will now allow me to walk out and stand beneath an extraordinary welcome. Ten times my height. Deeply familiar-feeling yet utterly strange. A sign from heaven, left here for our human puzzling. A swift succession of pen-strokes, making a mystical addition to the alphabet. Painted orange, like the rest of the site, but on an altogether larger scale, with the slash-scoop of the roof supported on two colossal and immensely old tree-trunks. I run my eyes over them carefully, then my hands. Patched and repaired with parts of other and younger trees, they create a magnificent beginning – a gateway to the island and the self. And because the *torii* gives such a complex address to the spirit, it makes a heartening departure-point as well. A high and apparently empty space through which I pass in wonder, marvelling at the sense of mystery it encloses, and at the evidence of common humanity as well: the tokens that others before me have pressed into the ancient wood, and to which I now add, delving into my pocket and finding a coin which is suddenly transformed into a prayer to leave behind me, and a wish to keep with me.

ABOVE AND LEFT: The *torii* gateway to the Itsukushima Shrine. At high tide the structure is immersed in water and appears to float; at low tide visitors can walk through it.

Maharashtra, India

ELLORA CAVES

Carved between ca. 600 and ca. 1000 CE into the basalt cliffs some 20 miles (30 km) from the city of Aurangabad in western India, the 34 caves of Ellora extend over more than a mile. They are a lasting monument to the remarkable spirit of tolerance among the Subcontinent's three great indigenous faiths: Buddhism, Jainism and Hinduism.

Most of these so-called "caves" have several chambers, each one hewn from the solid rock. The twelve Buddhist caves were carved in the early 7th century, and are mostly monasteries (*viharas*), built on several storeys with dormitories and kitchens as well as shrine rooms and assembly halls (*chaityas*). The monks who once lived here are now long gone, but a contemplative stillness still reigns in the abandoned cells and rooms where they would have gathered for meditation, teaching and worship. The *chaitya* of Cave 10 is a place of hushed tranquillity, where a colossal seated Buddha looks down from his throne beneath a beamed ceiling convincingly carved to look like wood. Cave 6 has a beautiful statue of Tara, the *bodhisattva* of compassion, her serene face embodying the deity's superhuman kindness.

Five Jain caves are smaller in scale, but here, too, are lively and exquisite carvings and sculptures, such as the deity Ambika sitting on a lion beneath a mango tree in Cave 34.

At the heart of the seventeen Hindu caves is the magnificent Kailash Temple (Cave 16). Begun in the 700s and dedicated to the god Shiva, this breathtaking complex of monumental gateways, spacious courtyards and halls,

intimate shrine rooms and soaring towers was sculpted from one enormous rock set in the basalt cliffs.

The range of sculpture is astonishing, from massive freestanding elephants to exquisitely detailed and energetic friezes of Shiva, his consort Parvati and a host of other deities. These sculptures were originally decorated in rich colours (some still bear traces of the paint), while the main tower was once plastered white in imitation of the sacred snows of Mount Kailash, home of Lord Shiva.

BELOW, LEFT: The Kailash Temple at the Ellora Caves. Hewn from a single rock in the basalt cliffs of Maharashtra, the Hindu temple was designed as a stylized representation of the sacred peak of Mount Kailash (*see p165*).

BELOW: One of the five delicately carved Jain caves in the Ellora complex, which also includes twelve Buddhist caves and seventeen Hindu examples.

Bihar, India

THE BODHI TREE

Sometime around 500BCE an Indian prince named Siddhartha Gautama renounced his life of royal luxury and embarked on a spiritual quest to discover the root of human sufferings. Shaving his head and adopting beggar's robes, he left his palace in the Himalayan foothills and lived first as a hermit, then as a pupil of a Brahmin master. Still dissatisfied, Siddhartha joined five ascetics and for six years pursued a life of harsh austerities until, emaciated and close to death, he decided to follow a gentler path. He ate some rice, wove himself a simple mat of grass, and sat down to meditate at the base of a pipal, a variety of fig tree, determined to remain there until he found the insights he was seeking. These insights came after 49 days beneath the tree. From this moment he is known not as Siddhartha but as the "Enlightened One" – the Buddha – and the tree under which he sat is known as the Bodhi Tree, or Tree of Enlightenment.

The descendant of the original Bodhi Tree still stands today in Bodh Gaya near Patna in India's present-day Bihar Province. The world's oldest documented tree, it is the focal point for the many thousands of Buddhist pilgrims who come every year to pray and meditate at the site of the Buddha's enlightenment. The town of Bodh Gaya itself grew up around the tree, its many Buddhist temples and monuments including the famous 180 feet (55 metre) high Mahabodhi (Great Enlightenment) Temple of ca. 500CE, which towers alongside the Bodhi Tree and inspired other monuments all over the Buddhist world. The tree was twice maliciously cut down in antiquity, but each time it revived from the stump. The ancient and much-decayed tree finally blew down in a storm in 1876, but the present tree was grown from one of its seeds, a testament to the endurance and regenerative capacity of the Buddha's teachings.

RIGHT: A Buddhist monk praying before the sacred Bodhi Tree under which the Buddha gained enlightenment.

BELOW: Buddha statues carved into the base of the Mahabodhi Temple. The Bodhi Tree is situated at its northeastern corner.

Shanxi, China

YUNGANG CAVE SHRINES

A stretch of rugged sandstone cliffs along the Wuzhou river valley, not far from the present-day city of Datong, is home to one of the world's most remarkable Buddhist monuments. Running for more than half a mile along the river, the cliffs were selected in ca. 460CE by the emperor Wencheng of the Northern Wei dynasty for a network of more than 250 exquisitely decorated Buddhist cave shrines. Appalled by the violent anti-Buddhist policies of his predecessor, Wencheng employed tens of thousands of craftsmen to hew the grottoes from the solid rock as a monumental act of piety.

Many of the artists who created the Yungang grottoes came directly from working on the similar Buddhist caves in the far west of China, at the Silk Road site of Mogao, where they worked in styles derived from Central Asia and India, the homeland of Buddhism. These influences can be seen at Yungang, representing the peak of early Chinese Buddhist art, and the start of a transitional phase to more purely Chinese styles. Imperial patronage ended in 494CE when the Northern Wei decamped to Luoyang, hundreds of miles to the south, and the artists and sculptors of Yungang soon left to work on a new cave complex at Longmen, near the new capital. From then on, Yungang was left to the monks, pilgrims and, today, tourists.

These intricately sculpted and painted grottoes contain more than 50,000 statues and reliefs, from colossal fierce Buddhist guardians to miniature Buddhas seated serenely in delicately ornamented niches, framed by lotus petals, flames and countless spiritual beings. Some of the niches are carved to resemble the elaborate, long-decayed wooden façades that once formed the entrance to the grottoes. While some façades were replaced in later centuries, most of the grottoes are now open to the elements. Despite this, and the present-day threat from sandstorms caused by deforestation, many of the figures retain their brilliant, vibrant colours after 1,500 years.

ABOVE AND LEFT: Buddha statues in the grottoes of Yungang, carved in their thousands in the 5th and 6th centuries CE as a great act of piety. Much of the stone surrounding these statues has weathered away, leaving them exposed.

RIGHT: A Sufi woman worshipping at the wall of the Dargah of Nizamuddin. Devotees tie pieces of red string to this latticework to remind the saint of their prayers.

BELOW: Qawwali musicians play Sufi devotional music at the tomb.

New Delhi, India

DARGAH OF NIZAMUDDIN

BY MARK TULLY

Sufi symbol of universal faith

Enmity between different faiths seems to me to be contrary to their spirit and gives ammunition to those who vociferously defame religion. That is why I have such respect for the *dargah*, or shrine, of the 13th-century mystic Hazrat Nizamuddin Auliya who is one of south Asia's most revered Sufi saints.

Sufism is an Islamic tradition, which teaches those who adopt its way to realize their inner selves. Rumi, the Sufi poet so popular today, said, "Sufism is the effort of man to reunite with the understanding from which he has been cut off." That understanding has much in common with the understanding sought by mystic traditions of other religions. They are the traditions that concentrate on experiencing God, or the transcendental, rather than emphasizing creeds and moral codes. So Sufism stands for what faiths have in common rather than their differences.

Nizamuddin's shrine is a symbol of this unity. In the crowded narrow lanes surrounding the shrine, stalls sell traditional Muslim food – mutton kebabs cooked on makeshift grills and steaming mounds of biryani. All the requirements for worship at Muslim shrines – red rose petals, prayer caps, beads, joss sticks and much else – are on sale too. But Hindus, Sikhs and Christians as well as Muslims find their way to this shrine.

Inside the shrine, which is set in a walled compound, those who have come to pray and seek the blessing of Hazrat Nizamuddin Auliya are expected to pay their obeisance first at the tomb of his most renowned disciple, the poet Amir Kushro. Nizamuddin's tomb itself, which has been rebuilt and modified several times over the centuries, is a white marble structure capped by a white onion dome with black marble stripes. Next to the shrine stands an original 13th-century red sandstone mosque with three flatter domes. A veranda supported by marble pillars and arches with delicate inlaid flowers and Arabic inscriptions surrounds the chamber where the tomb stands. Those who have come with a specific request tie pieces of red string on the latticework of the chamber's wall to remind Hazrat Nizamuddin Auliya of the blessing they have asked for or the help they have sought. Inside the chamber worshippers shower red rose petals on the green sheet draped over the tomb, kiss the railings surrounding it and, if they are Muslims, recite the first verse of the Quran. Every Thursday evening except in Ramadan, the Muslim month of fasting, people of all faiths and of none come to hear a group of Qawwali (Sufi devotional) musicians sing the praises of Allah and the saint in the quadrangle in front of the tomb. The zeal and the zest of Qawwali singing are so overpowering that the music is said to have rendered one of the other great Indian Sufi saints unconscious with rapture as he listened.

Behind the shrine of the 13th-century saint stands the shrine of a 20th-century Sufi saint, the renowned musician Inayat Khan. He once said, "All religions taught by Christ or any of the great ones were intended to awaken in man that sense which is awakened when religion is living." Inayat Khan founded what he called Universal Worship, not to create a new religion but to bring different religions together. So for me the shrines of Hazrat Nizamuddin Auliya and Inayat Khan stand for a religion that allows me to continue in the Anglican tradition in which I was born and yet be part of the universal faith that underlies the teachings of all those who have realized their inner selves.

Quảng Ninh, Vietnam

HA LONG BAY

According to one Vietnamese legend, the 1,600 limestone islands of Ha Long Bay were once precious jewels, spat out from a celestial dragon's mouth in a bid to repel an invading fleet. According to another tale, Ha Long was created by the beast's thrashing tail digging out deep valleys and crevices in the mainland, which were then filled up by the sea. And for anyone first coming across this felicitous conjunction of sparkling blue water and bright green, foliage-clad limestone crags, it does indeed look like the product of some divine force.

Each island or outcrop has its own unique shape. Some look for all the world like animals: there's a Voi (Elephant) island and a Ga Choi (Fighting Cock), as well as Dog, Turtle and Toad rocks. Some islands have internal lakes, some have spectacular caves and grottoes at their core, such as the spectacular Hang Dau Go (Wooden Stakes Cave), which boasts a forest of stalactites and stalagmites, many bearing a resemblance to birds, beasts and humans. And Trinh Nu (Virgin Cave) marks the lonely prison of a young girl who, so legend has it, was given to a wealthy merchant, to repay a debt owed by her parents; her refusal of her master's advances led to her being incarcerated on the tiny island, where she pined away (for love of her young fisherman boyfriend) and eventually turned to stone.

It is said that, to this day, the dragon dwells beneath the waters of Ha Long Bay, and for the inhabitants of its floating villages, many of whom have never set foot on land, each fishing expedition begins with a placatory offering to the seafaring deities. This small, personal ceremony takes place quietly and out of view of visitors, in one of the many hundreds of private shrines that have been hollowed out of the islands' stone over the centuries.

RIGHT: Some of the 1,600 limestone crags of Ha Long Bay, each one formed over millions of years. Ha Long means "dragon descending" and various legends involving this mythical beast are associated with the bay's creation.

New Delhi, India

BAHÁ'Í LOTUS TEMPLE

The Bahá'í faith was founded in the 19th century by an Iranian nobleman, Bahá'u'lláh, who proclaimed the essential unity of all religions. So when Iranian-born architect Fariborz Sahba was commissioned in the early 1980s to design a new mother temple for the Indian Bahá'í community, he sought to create a building that was unique yet familiar, strikingly modern but also reflecting India's rich spiritual and cultural heritage. The only stipulation was that the new temple, or House of Worship, should have nine sides in accordance with Bahá'í tradition. For Bahá'ís, nine signifies completion, and the nine-pointed star is a common symbol of the Bahá'í faith.

Inspiration for the new temple eventually came in the form of the lotus flower, or water lily, which symbolizes creation, enlightenment and the purified soul. The "Lotus Temple" rises from beautiful landscaped gardens like a great blossom unfolding to the sun. Encircled by nine pools, the structure appears to float ethereally on water.

The interior is a plain and tranquil space, bathed in the diffused sunlight that filters through 27 marble-clad "petals". Bahá'í temples welcome people of all faiths and of none, and the Lotus Temple has an entrance at each of its nine sides to symbolize this openness to all world-views. Bahá'ís believe that we must seek truth and God for ourselves, not blindly follow the dogmas and traditions of others, so there are no priests, altars, pulpits or images. Nor are there prescribed rites or acts of worship. In the temple anyone may recite prayers or read from Bahá'í scriptures in relaxed but dignified gatherings. A perfect combination of spiritual function and inspirational design, the Lotus Temple is not the home of formal rituals, but a place of fellowship for open hearts and minds.

LEFT: The striking, serene form of the Lotus Temple reflects the Bahá'í faith's emphasis on unity, acceptance and personal prayer.

RIGHT: A cave, probably a monk's dwelling, at the 12th-century ruins of Arankale Monastery. Little is known of the monastery's history, but the remains of various structures, including a bathing pool, promenades for walking meditations and a refectory, still lie among the trees of the forest.

BELOW: The *jantagara* or hot baths of the monastery.

North Western Province, Sri Lanka

ARANKALE FOREST MONASTERY

BY MICHAEL ONDAATJE

A stage beyond passion

At the entrance to Arankale a curved road of sand will lead you into the forest. A monk sweeps his way along the path for two hours each morning, removing a thousand leaves. By late afternoon another thousand leaves and light twigs have fallen upon it. But at noon its surface is as clear and yellow as a river. To walk this sand path is itself an act of meditation.

The forest is so still that you hear no sounds until you think of listening for them. Then you locate the noisemakers in the landscape, as if using a sieve in water, catching the calls of the orioles and parrots. It is said that "those who cannot love make places like this. One needs to be in a stage beyond passion."

Gradually you discover a bathing pool, the remnants of many sites, and then a clearing, like a *kamatha*, the threshing circle in a paddy field, where there is a small temple. On a ledge of stone rests a small statue of the Buddha, a cut plantain leaf protecting him from glare and rain. Here, the forest towers over you as though you are within a deep green well. The corrugated overhang by a nearby cave to keep out sun and rain rattles and shakes whenever the wind comes down through the trees.

Kings and those who are powerful desire what weighs them to the ground. Historical honour, measured ownership, their sure truths. But in Arankale, in the last years of the 12th century, Asanga the Wise and his followers lived for decades in solitude, the world unaware of them. When they died this forest monastery was stilled of humans. And in those uninhabited years, the paths were leaf-filled, there was

no song of sweeping. No odour of saffron or margosa came from the baths. Arankale perhaps became more beautiful, and more subtle without humans in the structure they had designed when they were no longer in the currents of love.

Not until four centuries later did monks begin living again in the caves above what had once been the temple clearing. It had been a long era of humanlessness, religiouslessness. The knowledge of such a monastery had vanished from people's minds and the site was an abandoned forest sea. What was left of wooden altars was eaten by colonies of insects. Generations of pollen silted the bathing pool and then rough vegetation consumed it, so it was invisible to any passer-by who did not know its sudden loose depth, which was a haven for creatures that scurried on the warmth of the cut rock and on unnamed plants in the nocturnal world.

For four hundred years the unheard throat calls of birds. The hum of some medieval bee motoring itself into the air. And in the remnant of the 12th-century well, under the reflected sky, a twist of something silver in the water.

South Korea

CHEJU ISLAND

An oval of rock with a volcano at its centre, Cheju Island sits in the shimmering turquoise ocean, just south of the Korean peninsula. The crater-marked hills once spewed flows of lava, whose legacies are some of the longest underground lava-tunnels in the world.

The culture of the island's inhabitants is quite distinct from that of mainland Korea. The local folklore is rich, describing more than 18,000 deities, and temples are plentiful. Among them the temple at Samyang, decorated with vibrant colours and patterns, stands on top of a hill offering a stunning panorama which stretches from the ocean to Cheju City. Villagers protect themselves from bad luck by piling stones into small towers known as *bangsatap*, while basalt-carved *dolhareubang*, or "stone grandfathers" (*below*),

are thought to ward off evil, and stand in line at certain places all over the island.

The Gotjawal Forest, which grows up the slopes of the volcano Mount Halla, is home to an astounding selection of unique plant and animal life. Indeed, in Chinese mythology, Cheju is home to a mushroom that bestows immortality.

According to legend, the Goddess of Creation made Mount Halla with the earth from seven digs of her spade, and it is unsurprising that the people of an island linked to this powerful goddess have a matriarchal tradition. Cheju is home to the *haenyeo* – "sea women" who dive for abalone and mother of pearl, as breadwinners for their families. Although now a rarity, it is still possible to see women diving into the ocean, and then rising, goddess-like with iridescent shells in their hands.

Shaolin, China
PAGODA FOREST

At the foot of Shaosi Mountain, near the Shaolin Monastery, stands a monumental living graveyard to Buddhism: the largest pagoda forest in China.

Standing amid the majestic, wooded hills of Henan Province, on the plain between the Yellow and Huaihe rivers, the "forest" consists of around 250 stone or brick towers, each containing the ashes of a famous or high-ranking monk of the nearby temple. The earliest, cracked and leaning to one side, dates from 791CE, during the Tang Dynasty; others have been added throughout the centuries, right up to the present day. Indeed, one of the most recent pagodas, carved in 2002, shows images of a car, video camera and laptop – all possessions of the deceased monk.

Although the tottering structures look haphazard, certain aspects of their form are in fact dictated by strict rules. Each pagoda has an odd number of storeys (one, three, five or seven), the number of levels being proportionate to the achievements of the monk for whom the pagoda was built.

Right at the centre of the group stands the famous Yugong Pagoda. Its seven storeys were built in the 14th century to commemorate the life of the monk Fu Yu, granted the title of duke by the Yuan emperor, the only monk in the history of the Shaolin Monastery to be awarded such an honour.

The Yugong Pagoda is hexagonal, but some of the pagodas are square, others cylindrical, conical, monolithic or even vase-shaped, depending on the era in which they were built. Mostly stone or brick, they are often inscribed with calligraphy, and are valuable records of the development of artistic style and craftsmanship through China's dynasties.

Each of these monuments should be viewed as a memorial to a soul, so that as they multiply, seemingly organically, the forest bears witness to a litany of religious lives.

Lhasa Prefecture, Tibet

LHASA

BY PAUL THEROUX

Town of pilgrims, prayer wheels and snowy peaks

Lhasa is a small, friendly-looking town on a high plain surrounded by even higher mountains. There is very little traffic. There are no pavements. Everyone walks in the street. No one runs. These streets are at 12,000 feet. You can hear children yelling and dogs barking and bells being rung, and so it seems a quiet place. Every street has a vista of tremendous Tibetan mountains.

Lhasa is a holy place, so it is populated by pilgrims. These pilgrims hunker and prostrate themselves all over Lhasa, and they shuffle clockwise around every shrine. They flatten themselves on stair-landings, outside the Jokhang and all around the Potala. They do it on the road, the riverbank, the hillsides. They pray, they throw themselves to the ground, and they strew tiny one-*miao* notes and barley grains at the shrines, and they empty blobs of yak butter into the lamps. Being Tibetan Buddhists they are good-humoured and because

they are from all over Tibet, Lhasa is their meeting-place – they enrich the life of the town and fill its markets. They come out of a devotion to the Dalai Lama, the incarnation of the *bodhisattva* Avalokitesvara. Pilgrims have made Lhasa a town of visitors who are not exactly strangers, and so even a real foreigner feels a sense of belonging there. Its chaos and dirt and its jangling bells make it seem hospitable.

When I visited the Jokhang, Tibet's holiest place, I arrived near the end of Tibetan New Year, a fifteen-day festival known both for its piety and its rambunctiousness. The monks – about a thousand or more – had gathered to chant mantras. They were all ages – some were no more than teenagers – and some were women, but they had shaven heads and were robed like men, and so they were almost indistinguishable. I watched it all from an upper balcony, where Tibetans tossed scraps of paper with mantras written on them to the monks below, who made piles of them. Tibetan pilgrims thronged the Jokhang, muttering prayers, prostrating themselves, and gawking at the monks. Their eyes glittered in the half-dark of the cloisters and these people took on the odd curiosity of tourists with their squints and stares, as if, so startled were they by the droning monks and the aromas and the drooping *tanka*s, they had forgotten to pray.

All this time, everywhere in Lhasa, the prayer wheels were spinning. The pilgrims plodded clockwise and spun the wheels – often very quickly, because the prayers uttered by each wheel (there is a scribbled mantra inside) are weaker than spoken prayers. Some wheels were the size of oil drums and very hard to turn, others were no larger than nail kegs, and you could hear the flutter of the mantras in their innards as they spun. They were all inscribed in Tibetan and Sanskrit with the efficacious mantra *om mani padmi hum* – the *om* is the most powerful and mystical element in the mantra, a combination of three Sanskrit sounds that sum up the

ABOVE: The Potala Palace, formerly the chief residence of the Dalai Lama, as seen from Jokhang Temple.

LEFT: A monk plays a ceremonial trumpet (*dung*), while others chant and offer prayers at the Jokhang, considered the most sacred site in all of Tibet.

FAR LEFT: A line of prayer wheels inscribed with the mantra *om mani padmi hum*. Spinning a wheel, usually clockwise, is considered to have much the same effect as saying a prayer out loud.

three-in-one nature of the universe. These prayers are so sacred that just writing them or carving them in stone (the sacred *om* is frequently seen hacked into cliff-faces) is regarded as much more pious than putting up statues.

An early European explorer to Tibet burst into tears when he saw one lovely mountain covered in snow. That did not seem to me an odd reaction. The setting is more than touching – it is a bewitchment: the light, the air, the emptiness, the plains and peaks. Dusty crags and steep slopes surround Lhasa, and on some mornings I was there they were covered in snow from flurries in the night. The snow represents holiness and purity to the Tibetans, whose glissading spirits need this symbol of innocence to prove they are still free: such snowy mountains are proof of God's existence.

When I left Tibet I lifted up my eyes to the mountains and clasped my hands and invented a clumsy prayer that went: Please let me come back.

LEFT: Prayer flags fluttering at dawn, with the roof of the Jokhang Temple behind.

Angkor, Cambodia

ANGKOR WAT

At Angkor, the seat of the Khmer Empire for more than 600 years, Buddhist and Hindu rulers created extraordinary monuments that expressed their belief in a divinely ordained cosmic order which they, as *devarajas* ("god-kings"), played an essential role in maintaining. Among these sacred monuments is the temple of Angkor Wat, probably the most magnificent Hindu temple outside India itself.

Built by Suryavarman II (ruled 1113–50), Angkor Wat was dedicated to the god Shiva, preserver of the cosmos and upholder of universal order. It was, therefore, constructed as a three-dimensional map of the cosmos. Surrounded by a vast ritual purification pool that symbolizes the primordial waters around the world, the temple stands on an artificial island that represents the Earth, which Hindu cosmology envisions as square. Rising above the waters are the temple's five typically Khmer "corn-cob" *prang*s (towers). These represent the mountain homes of the gods, with the great central tower – formerly accessible only to priests and kings – representing the mystic Mount Meru, the abode of Shiva and centre of the universe (*see p165*). Angkor Wat faces west, which is unusual for Hindu temples, but it means that anyone approaching the temple at dawn on midsummer's day will see the sun apparently rising from the top of the central tower. It is surely no coincidence that the name of the *devaraja* Suryavarman means "protector sun".

Amid the stunning monumentality of the temple's overall scheme are the smaller-scale glories of its sculptures. These include the world's longest series of carved reliefs, executed for the edification of the faithful and depicting gods and other beings in vivid scenes from Hindu creation mythology.

Angkor Wat is approached by a 650-feet (200-metre) bridge across the waters that surround it. For the modern visitor, no less than for worshippers of old, this physical separation from the everyday world creates a powerful sense that to enter the temple is to embark on a sacred journey – a pilgrimage to the realm of the gods.

PREVIOUS PAGES AND FAR LEFT, ABOVE: The vast Angkor Wat temple complex. Based on the ancient Hindu vision of the cosmos, the temple's five "corn-cob" towers represent the mountain homes of the gods.

FAR LEFT, BELOW: Graceful *apsara*s (celestial dancers), carved into the temple walls.

LEFT: Enormous stone faces at Bayon Temple, just north of Angkor Wat. Surveying the surrounding landscape in all directions, the faces are thought to be representations of the *bodhisattva* Avalokitesvara.

Himachal Pradesh, India

JANOG & THE TEMPLES OF HIMACHAL PRADESH

Experiencing the divine in the Himalayas

BY MARK TULLY

LEFT: The steps and simple stone plinth base of the village temple at Janog.

FAR LEFT: The seemingly never-ending ranges of the Himalayas in Himachal Pradesh, home to many remote villages, each with its own temple and presiding deity.

In India, the western Himalayan state of Himachal Pradesh is known as the Abode of the Gods, and those Gods have more than 2,000 temples to live in. The stone temples of Chamba, and the temple known as Jawalamukhi, or the Mouth of Flame, are famous, and very much on the tourist trail. But almost every village has its own small temple, each one unique in its design.

These are rarely visited, except by art historians and students of architecture like the architects Shabbir Khambatty and Swapnil Bhole who agreed to share their unpublished research and photographs with me. They have helped me to understand the connection between nature and the village temples of Himachal Pradesh. Being made of local wood and stone, the temples don't obtrude but fit into their surroundings – the sacred mountains of Himachal Pradesh, which unfold range after range like the waves of the sea until they come to the highest mountains of them all, the snow-capped Himalayan peaks. Each village temple has its own presiding deity closely connected with nature, celebrated in festivals which mark the passing of the seasons, and invoked for protection from the earthquakes the fragile mountains are prone to.

You do not have to drive far outside Shimla, the former summer capital of the British Raj and now the capital of Himachal Pradesh, to find these village temples. Only about 200 people live in the village of Janog, less than 25 miles (40 km) from Shimla, but they have their own temple and their own presiding deity. The temple, some 35 feet (10 metres) high, stands at the end of the village, overlooking a valley thousands of feet below. Its base is a stone plinth on which stand two simple rooms made of wood. The upper room is the *sanctum sanctorum*, the home of the deity. The walls of the tower are decorated with fringes of small, delicately carved wooden slats that sway in the breeze to make soft music. Sadly, the original sloping slate roof of the temple, which blended with the grey-green mountainside, has been replaced with corrugated tin. But the *poojari* or priest continues to recite the same prayers and perform the same rituals that have linked the villagers of Janog with their God down the centuries. Through their God they express the awe that the mountains, which are their home, inspire. He is also a homely God whom they can approach for protection, and celebrate in their joyful festivals

For me, the temples of Himachal Pradesh are symbols in wood and stone of the reverence one feels in the Himalayas. When I look out over those ranges I am sometimes overcome by a sense of a presence I can only call God. It's a humbling experience because the God I experience is infinitely greater than myself, but it's also a comforting experience because I feel at one with that God. In the Himalayas I often think of Gerard Manley Hopkins' well-known poem, "The Grandeur of God". The Jesuit poet is in awe of God's creation and shocked by our disrespect for its grandeur. He says, "all is seared with trade; bleared, smeared with toil; and wears man's smudge and shares man's smell". Yet he is confident that whatever we do, nature "is never spent". And why not? The poet says "Because the Holy Ghost over the bent / World broods with warm breast and with ah! bright wings."

For Christians the Holy Ghost is the guardian of nature and the God I experience in the Himalayas. The villagers who live in these mountains have their own guardians, their own Gods housed in their temples.

Shandong, China

MOUNT TAI

Standing roughly to the north, south, east and west of China's northern plains, four sacred mountains mark out the ancient heartland of the Middle Kingdom. But Chinese tradition also acknowledges a fifth direction – the cosmic "centre" – in addition to the usual four, so there are not merely four sacred peaks but five. The fifth and central mountain is Mount Tai or *Taishan*, the "Great Mountain". It has been China's holiest mountain and a pilgrimage site for as long as 3,000 years.

Mountains are revered in China as places of special power, the abodes of the Blessed Immortals and symbols of stability, strength, power and eternity. Where someone in the West might describe something as being "steady as a rock", the Chinese will say it is as "steady as Mount Tai". Rulers and ordinary people alike have come to worship at this peak. Over the centuries some 72 emperors made the pilgrimage to Mount Tai, where they worshipped the gods and prayed for prosperity at the imperial Dai Miao Temple at its foot. Now surrounded by the city of Tai'an, the temple was built to resemble an imperial palace and covers nearly 300,000 square feet (28,000 square metres).

There are many other shrines along the pilgrim paths that snake from Tai'an up the mountain's slopes, such as the Divine Rock Temple, known for the many statues in its Thousand Buddha Hall. But auspicious red streamers and countless other small offerings bear witness to the holiness of the entire mountainside. Not only are its temples, shrines and inscribed memorial tablets considered significant, but also natural features such as a 2,200-year-old tree and the Bridge of the Immortals, a cluster of boulders that forms precarious-looking stepping stones across a vertiginous ravine.

One of the world's longest flights of steps – around 7,000 of them – leads to the mountain's highest temple, known as the Azure Cloud Temple. The views from the top are breathtaking. Here, on the peak of Mount Tai, it is easy to imagine – as thousands of Chinese pilgrims have believed before you – that you have reached the abode of the Jade Emperor, the ruler of heaven itself.

Beijing, China

TEMPLE OF HEAVEN

Stand before the buildings that make up the Temple of Heaven complex and you will see the embodiment of humankind's desire for order amid earthly chaos. The perfect manifestation of this is the Hall of Prayer for Good Harvests (*right*). A perfectly symmetrical structure, it consists of three upturned, dark blue-glazed saucers, separated by bands of ornate, pale blue-and-gold carving, and topped by a gilded sphere. Its architecture is infused with precise symbolism. Inside, three rings of columns hold up the blue-tiled roof, an embodiment of the sky. Four columns at the centre represent the four seasons, twelve in the next ring represent the twelve months of the year and twelve outer columns the twelve hours of the daytime. The entire building is also, by virtue of its circular shape, a symbol of heaven itself.

It was to this building that the emperor of China, himself known as the Son of Heaven, would come in solemn procession on the eve of the winter solstice to pray for healthy crops and to meditate in the adjoining Imperial Vault of Heaven, a scaled-down version of the Hall of Prayer. The next day he would return, to perform ritual sacrifices and prayers on the Circular Mound Altar, a three-tiered marble terrace in the same complex. Again, symbolism plays a crucial part in the design: the number of flagstones in every circle of the Mound's three-tiered terrace is a multiple of nine – the imperial number. The harvest ceremony had to be performed without a hitch. According to tradition, the slightest mistake on the emperor's part was a bad omen for the nation's well-being over the coming year.

Contemplating the symbolism and symmetry captured in these buildings, you glimpse a respect for form and tradition that was not mere superstition, but active worship. At the same time, the sounds of secular China provide the modern-day visitor with a more earthly counterpoint: laughing teenagers experimenting with the Imperial Vault of Heaven's echo wall, while the voices of their elders waft over from morning choral practice in the surrounding park, singing old favourites from the Communist songbooks.

Java, Indonesia

BOROBUDUR

Built in the 8th and 9th centuries by the Sailendra dynasty, the great Buddhist monument of Borobudur was hidden by ash for more than 800 years after the nearby Mount Merapi erupted in 1006. Known as the "Ineffable Mountain of Accumulated Virtues", the structure is a stepped pyramid of square platforms for worshippers to process around clockwise as they climb to the summit. It is located in a sacred area of the city of Magelang in Central Java known as Kedu Plain, an elevated platform situated between two rivers and two volcanoes, and remains a hugely popular site of Buddhist pilgrimage today.

Rising against a backdrop of mountains and jungle, Borobudur is a vast, three-dimensional model of the cosmos, adorned with relief panels, Buddha statues and stupas. The original purpose of Borobudur is unclear: some see it as a temple, some as a funerary monument, others as an enormous stupa. Six square-shaped platforms, their four sides facing the four cardinal directions, support three circular tiers, which culminate in a large central stupa. Seen from above, the plan can also be understood as a giant mandala – a stylized diagram of a perfect universe.

A visit to Borobudur is a symbolic, circumambulatory pilgrimage, known as a *pradaksina*, to the sacred summit. The terraces act as pathways, guiding pilgrims around the structure in a clockwise direction as they ascend to each new tier by way of stone staircases. The climb is enlivened by thousands of intricate bas-relief panels, designed to be read from right to left as pilgrims circle the monument. The panels relay complex narratives from the Life and Past Lives of the Buddha from the *Lalitavistara* and *Jataka* stories, as well as the story of Sudhana, a young Buddhist disciple who achieved enlightenment. Graceful stone *apsara*s drift by on clouds, kings and queens hold court in sumptuous surroundings and lively musicians play delicately carved flutes and gongs. This

LEFT: A broken stupa reveals a meditating stone Buddha. Each of the 72 miniature stupas on the upper level of Borobudur contains a Buddha sculpture.

great ascent has been practised by devotees for centuries and is said to symbolize the spiritual path of the *bodhisattva* toward enlightenment and nirvana.

On climbing the final staircase, the pilgrim reaches the uppermost level of the structure, the realm of enlightenment, awakening and Buddhahood. Here, overlooking the lush surrounding jungles and the sacred volcano Mount Merapi, 72 miniature stupas surround a central stupa in perfectly orchestrated circles. Each of these smaller stupas is perforated to allow just a glimpse of the meditating stone Buddha that sits calmly within. Today some of the stupas are damaged, revealing the Buddha sculptures in their entirety. The four tiers of these stupas are said to represent the four immaterial levels of meditation.

To this day, each year Indonesian Buddhists celebrate Waisak – commemorating the birth, enlightenment and death of the Buddha – by processing to the summit of Borobudur.

ABOVE: The view from the uppermost level of the structure, looking out over the surrounding jungle.

RIGHT: Viewing Borobudur from above reveals its mandala-like structure.

Amritsar, India

GOLDEN TEMPLE

BY MARK TULLY

Reverence that cannot be hushed

Amritsar is to Sikhs what Jerusalem is to Christians, Mecca to Muslims, and Varanasi or Benares to Hindus – their most important place of pilgrimage. The Golden Temple is the heart of the Sikhs' sacred city.

First built in the 15th century by the Sikhs' fifth Guru, Arjan Dev, twice destroyed by Afghan invaders, the Golden Temple was rebuilt when the Afghans left in the 17th century and decorated as it stands today in the 18th century during the reign of the only Sikh Emperor, Ranjit Singh. The temple doesn't have the grandeur that their sheer size gives to some of the world's great religious monuments. Just 40½ feet square, the shrine's magnificence lies in its intricately decorated gilded bronze plating that gives the impression that it is built entirely of gold, gold that glitters in the water of the sacred pool the temple appears to be floating in. The architecture is ornate, too, with onion-shaped domes at each corner and a central gold-plated dome representing a lotus.

As pilgrims enter the white-walled complex surrounding the pool, the sound of hymns sung by musicians inside the temple floats across the water. Here they will prostrate themselves as a gesture of surrender to God – the Golden Temple is also known as Harimandir, or "God's abode". Some of these pilgrims will then sit on the edge of the pool quietly praying. Some will bathe in it. All will eventually walk around the pool to the causeway leading to the temple itself.

One of the Sikhs' fundamental beliefs is the equality of all, and so there are four doors to the temple symbolizing the principle that people from all corners of the world, no matter what their caste or creed, should be made welcome. The rise of Sikhism in the 16th century was in many ways akin to that century's Protestant revolution in Europe. Both grew out of a sense that religion had become encrusted by ritual and superstition, that priests had become too powerful,

ABOVE: Pilgrims visiting the Golden Temple light candles to show their devotion.

LEFT: Devotees queuing on the causeway between the mainland and the temple platform, which seems to float, weightless over the water.

and orthodoxy so important that it stifled spirituality. The founding gurus were teachers not priests, so Sikhs were taught they needed no Brahminical, sacerdotal intervention between them and their God. They didn't require the many gods of Hinduism as intermediaries between them and the ultimate being, any more than Protestants felt the intercession of saints was necessary. The last Guru told the Sikhs all the teaching they needed was contained in their scripture. The scripture was to be their Guru, and so was called the Guru Granth Sahib. As pilgrims enter the Golden Temple they prostrate themselves before the Granth Sahib, which is carried into the ornate *sanctum sanctorum* in a golden palanquin every morning.

Unlike so many shrines and places of worship in noisy, chaotic India, the Golden Temple complex is orderly. No pilgrims or other visitors are importuned by priests; the commercialism which goes with religious tourism is kept well away. The atmosphere is reverent but it is not the hushed reverence of a Christian church. Pilgrims and others chatter as they queue on the causeway that leads to the Golden Temple. Children aren't told that they are to be seen but not heard. The hymn singing is continuous; so are the readings from the scriptures.

But the Golden Temple is quintessentially Indian in that worshippers individually surrender to God, all seeking their own way to interpret the scriptures and experience the divine. There is no obligatory congregational worship, in fact there are no obligations beyond covering the head and behaving reverently. I'm not alone in feeling that the reverence, the hymns, the reflection of the Golden Temple shimmering in the water, the devotion of the volunteers on their knees swabbing the marble floors throughout the day, make the Golden Temple a place where it's almost impossible not to experience sacredness. That was why I was so distressed when, in 1984, the Golden Temple complex was desecrated by Sikh separatists who converted it into a fortress and invaded by the Indian army to remove them. But that sense of the sacred was soon restored.

LEFT: The shimmering gold exterior of the temple is intensified by its reflection in the water.

Kyoto, Japan

FUSHIMI INARI SHRINE

The mountain trails leading to the Fushimi Inari Shrine are sheltered by hundreds of tightly packed orange *torii* gates, creating several luminous miles of tunnelled pathways. These wooden *torii* are donated by devotees and are a traditional Shinto shrine feature, marking the entrance to a sacred space. According to custom, visitors wash their hands and mouth to cleanse themselves for this important transition from the secular to the sacred.

Nestled at the base of Mount Inari, this is one of the many Japanese shrines that celebrate the Shinto spirit Inari, who is associated with rice, fertility and prosperity. Inari is represented as either male or female, or sometimes as androgynous, and is one of the most popular spirits, or *kami*, among Shinto devotees.

At the bottom of the Inari hill are the *romon* (literally "main gate") and the *Go-Honden* ("main shrine"), which houses a symbolic Inari idol, a mirror. Behind them, in the middle of the mountain, is the *Oku miya* ("inner shrine"), reachable by a *torii*-lined path, and at the top of the mountain are tens of thousands of *tsuka* ("mounds") for private worship. Sculptures of *kitsune* ("foxes"), thought to be Inari's messengers, are found throughout the complex, often holding a key (to the rice granary), a scrolled business contract or a sheaf of rice in their mouth or paw.

Several million worshippers visit the shrine over the three-day Japanese New Year. Offerings of rice, sake and other food are given at the shrine to appease the *kitsune* messengers, who are then expected to plead with Inari on the worshipper's behalf. *Inari-zushi*, a Japanese sushi roll of fried tofu, is another popular offering as it is believed to be a favourite food of Japanese foxes.

RIGHT: One of the pathways to the Fushimi Inari Shrine, sheltered by orange *torii* gates that have been donated by Inari worshippers.

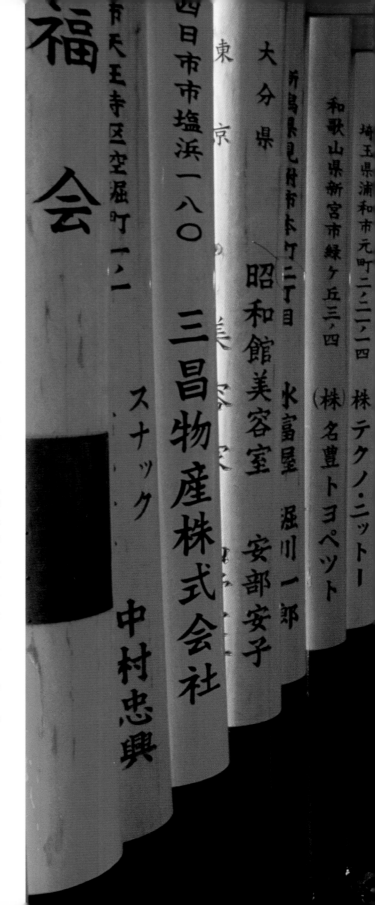

South Island, New Zealand

AORAKI/MOUNT COOK

Aoraki ("Cloud Piercer") rises 12,300 feet (3,700 metres) above sea level, making it New Zealand's highest mountain. More important to the Ngai Tahu people than its height, however, is that Aoraki is a monument to the first child of the god Raki, father of the sky, and his sky wife Poharua Te Po ("breath of life in the womb of darkness").

When Raki came to Earth to marry the Earth Mother, Papa-tui-nuku, his sky children came down from the heavens to pay homage to her. Aoraki and his three brothers, Rakiro, Rakiru and Rarakiroa, were turned into stone when their canoe capsized, as they tried to ascend back to the skies. The brothers, scrambling to the highest point of the wreckage, were frozen by the South Wind, and became the South Island. Now the triple-peaked Aoraki is surrounded by his brothers, in the form of Mounts Dampier, Tasman and Teichelmann, for eternity. The more scientific version of the story is that the mountains were made by tectonic uplifting along the Pacific and Indo-Australian plates. This pressure is ongoing, pushing the mountain range higher at the rate of ¼ inch (6 mm) per year.

In 1851, Captain John Stokes renamed Aoraki "Mount Cook" after James Cook, the first European to sail around the islands. In the intervening years the mountain has become a famous destination for outdoor pursuits. There are more than 300 species of plants in the National Park, including the mountain daisy and giant buttercups known as "Mount Cook lilies", and the mountain parrot, the jewelled gecko and the black stilt are among the rare creatures that inhabit the area.

For the Ngai Tahu, however, to climb the mountain would be sacrilegious. Aoraki is the physical embodiment of the greatest of their ancestors, and the link from this world to the supernatural.

LEFT: Aoraki/Mount Cook, at the centre left of the mountains in this picture, is believed to be the first child of the god Raki turned to stone.

The Kimberley, Australia

BUNGLE BUNGLE

The Aboriginal creation stories, the Dreamtime, describe the mythical process by which Australia was formed. These stories are bound to the physical appearance of the landscape – as though the need to explain topographical oddities sparked the imagination of the ancient race, and suggested to them a world of supernatural creator-beings.

Bungle Bungle, in Western Australia, is one of the "dreaming places" – areas that are home to the spirits of the Dreamtime. This massif is as pitted and cratered as a lunar landscape, and looking at the alien swellings and nodules of rock, striped in orange and grey, it is almost impossible to believe that they are the result of a natural phenomenon. In fact, these huge, banded beehives are the result of erosion. Centuries of hot wind from the Tanami Desert have exposed the sandstone and algae of the Earth's inner layers and created an oceanic landscape that, from the air, looks like a coral reef, its colours dazzling the eye in shades of azure and orange, emerald and indigo, gold and grey.

Echidna Gorge is a narrow chasm that slices through two of the massive red-gold sandstone cliffs. In some places, the gorge is only 7 feet (2 metres) wide but, at 1¼ miles (2 km) long, it looks as though some giant or god has taken his sword to the cliff over an ancient grievance.

The area contains some of the most spectacular wildlife in Australia – in particular, the many species of birds living along the dry riverbeds of the plateau. Budgerigars and rainbow bee-eaters flit along these creeks. Astonishingly, the area was not explored by non-Aboriginals until the 1980s, and is still very much the spiritual preserve of the Aboriginals. To visit Bungle Bungle today is to witness the tradition of the Dreamtime.

RIGHT AND ABOVE: The banded sandstone structures of the Bungle Bungle, formed by millions of years of weathering. The site is considered a "dreaming place" by the local Aboriginals.

Northern Territory, Australia

ULURU

BY PICO IYER

Australia's silent, pulsing heart

The Taj Mahal, the Pyramids at Giza, the Great Wall of China: all show what man can do to (and with) Nature; Uluru, long known to the Western world as Ayers Rock, shows you what Nature can do to man. It just stands there, an 1,100-foot (335-metre) "island mountain" rising out of absolute emptiness at the heart of Australia's "Red Centre", more than 200 miles from the nearest small town, in the southern part of the Northern Territory, and it says nothing. It offers no chambers or turrets or inscriptions. It simply confronts you, massive, implacable and Ozymandias-like, and asks you what you are doing with your life.

All the land of the world's oldest continent is sacred to its indigenous people, of course, a vast and complex network of songlines charting a secret geography illegible to foreigners. But Uluru has a special charge for the Aboriginal people who have lived around it for tens of thousands of years. For them it is filled with the spirits of dozens of creator beings. In one account, a small red lizard threw a curved stick into the great rock and died trying to take it out; in another, two blue-tongued lizard men killed an emu fleeing from the Bell-Bird brothers, and the rival bands of predators faced off at exactly this haunting spot.

Paintings in the caves around Uluru show stories of the Dreamtime, and the rock offers a permanent waterhole in the middle of the unforgiving desert. Modern visitors are asked not to climb the sacred structure, but many do, and many die each year in the attempt. Even taking pictures of certain parts of the great monolith – or taking away pieces of it – is regarded as a kind of profanation. For its Anangu caretakers, the whole area is alive.

To add to the magic, the sandstone of Uluru is constantly changing colour in the light, so that this most mute and immobile of presences seems to have a hundred selves. "This

ABOVE AND FOLLOWING PAGES, RIGHT: The great Uluru rock formation, iconic symbol of Australia, and of great sacred importance to the country's indigenous people.

LEFT: The rock has a high iron content, which has "rusted" to give it its deep red colour.

rock appears more wonderful every time I look at it," said William Gosse, one of the first European explorers to set eyes on it, in 1873. In its way it stands for all the pulsing potency of Australia's Interior, an elemental, haunted place of red-dirt paths and whitened trees, twisted at odd angles in the emptiness under a brilliant cobalt sky.

Uluru, in short, has a magnetism and a presence that no postcard or photograph can capture; it is the rare place with such charisma that it makes every report of it seem small. You can feel its immanence, shockingly, as you drive towards it, and long after you've left. It's easy, on first visiting Australia, to think that its blond-bright cities, its lifestyle comforts, its pretty, white-sand beaches speak for its special graces; but it is only when you travel into its heart that you see that its real power lies with silence and emptiness, its ancient stories of willie wagtails and feuding snakes.

The traditional indigenous name that has been restored to "Uluru" almost bears that out. It looks strange to most of us, and there's a "u" at its beginning, in its centre and at its end. In some ways, what the name is telling you is that this is the place where all words run out.

ABOVE: In the many caves surrounding Uluru, paintings depict scenes from the Dreamtime. These images are regularly freshened with new layers of paint.

Raiatea Island, French Polynesia

TAPUTAPUATEA

The Society Islands of French Polynesia, and in particular Raiatea Island, are believed to be the birthplace of Polynesian spiritual belief. In the Tahitian language, *raiatea* means "clear sky" and the island is an idyllic tropical paradise, adorned with wild hibiscus, bamboo, Tahitian chestnut and the rare delicate white flower known as *tiare apetahi*. The ancestors of the Polynesians, originating from Micronesia some 50,000 years ago, are thought to have settled on Raiatea first, and then sailed forth to populate vast tracts of the Pacific Ocean.

The ancient *marae* (an area cleared for ceremonial purposes) in the commune of Taputapuatea is the biggest and most important sacred site in Polynesia (*below*). Every five years, Polynesian peoples from as far as New Zealand, Easter Island and Hawaii still gather here to remember their common ancestors. A large standing stone at the centre of the *marae* creates a stark silhouette in the setting sun akin to that of an Easter Island statue. Around 1,500 years ago, this temple platform was built from coral and black volcanic rock by worshippers of the war and fertility god Oro, son of the creator god Ta'aroa and believed to have been born on the island. All other *marae* in Polynesia, even those as far away as New Zealand, are supposed to be built over a sacred stone from Taputapuatea or one of its descendent temples. The entire area surrounding Taputapuatea, including the crater of the Fa'arua volcano, is regarded as "sacred space" by the Polynesians, and Fa'arua Crater is known as the "navel of the world".

In ancient times, warriors living in the crater would descend to worship at the oceanside temple at Taputapuatea before setting off on their voyages of conquest, offering human and animal sacrifices before departing. For generations after them, Polynesians would have continued to seek the blessing of the chieftains of the temple before setting out to found dynasties in Hawaii, Samoa, Rarotonga (the Cook Islands) and New Zealand.

Queensland, Australia

CARNARVON GORGE

Carnarvon Gorge, a 39,000-acre section of Queensland's Carnarvon National Park, is a place of unique natural and spiritual significance to the local Bidjara and Karingbal Aboriginal peoples. To the Aboriginals, Carnarvon Gorge was a "power place" – a site of extraordinary energies and a gathering place for annual traditional ceremonies.

The gorge, in the eastern and most visited section of the park, was formed many millions of years ago from shale, sandstone and other sedimentary rock deposits. Walking along its floor, visitors can clearly see these different strata, particularly the layers of sandstone, that make up the spectacular landforms. The gorge experiences lower temperatures and greater rainfall than the surrounding arid highlands, making it seem like a welcoming green sanctuary, full of eucalyptus, acacia, pines and king ferns.

In the lower reaches of the gorge is a 200 feet (60 metre) long rock "gallery", known as the Art Gallery. Unique in its range and variety, the Aboriginal stencil art to be found here consists of boomerang paintings, more than 1,300 engravings and 600 stencilled designs, mainly of human hands and fertility symbols. Nearby, an enormous rock shelter named Cathedral Cave has similar stencils on its walls. Created by blowing ochre mixed with water over a shape held up against the rock, these imprints are thought to have been made as part of a spiritual ceremony, symbolizing a bonding between man and the rock. More than 3,500 years old, the red and yellow tones of their pigments still surprisingly vivid, the stencils are among the most sophisticated of their kind in the world.

The local Aboriginal peoples who made these stencils did not, however, live permanently in Carnarvon Gorge itself – perhaps to avoid being trapped there by enemies, but more likely because the land was considered so sacred it should only be traversed and not permanently occupied.

Tongariro National Park, New Zealand

MOUNT RUAPEHU

The volcanoes that form the Tongariro National Park, at the southern tip of the North Island of New Zealand, are said to have been born of the prayers of the ancient high priest Ngatoroirangi. Travelling toward Lake Taupo, he saw a range of peaks and resolved to climb them. Before he reached the summit, a great snowstorm overtook him, and the priest found himself trapped in a whirling web of Antarctic gales. Desperate and cold, he prayed to the lord of the fiery underworld, Ruamoko, and was rewarded with a gift of lava, which burst forth from Mount Ruapehu and spilled all the way to his feet in a pool that formed the Pacific rim of fire.

The Maori consider the mountains in the range that contains the peaks of Ruapehu, Tongariro and Ngauruhoe to be *wahi tapu* or sacred sites. The word *tapu* is the root of our "taboo", perhaps because places that have been classified *tapu* should not be explored, discussed, disturbed or even looked at according to the Maori tradition.

Mount Ruapehu is the largest volcano in the country and still active. Between its semi-regular eruptions (major ones usually occur twice in every century), rainwater and melted ice collect in its crater, forming a huge, acidic mineral lake. On the mountain's slopes are some even more spectacular masses of water: the Emerald Lakes. Filled with the melt waters from the ice floes on the higher peaks, the lakes are full of andesite minerals from the surrounding rock, which tint them extraordinary colours. Sometimes emerald, sometimes jade, turquoise or a rich algae-green, the lakes are constantly changing shape and size like the snow drifts that lie alongside them in the winter. The Maori revered these breathing, swelling bodies of heavenly water, attributing to them spiritual powers of the living gods and the energy of *mana*: the ability to inspire awe that should be experienced but never explained.

RIGHT: The Emerald Lakes on the slopes of the sacred volcano Mount Ruapehu. Andesite minerals give the water its extraordinarily vivid colours.

Northern Territory, Australia

KATA TJUTA

Kata Tjuta appears like a series of tremendous ripples in the silken fabric of the desert. These rocks tower over the surrounding landscape in a collection of powder-red domes, dominating the skyline.

Kata Tjuta lies 25 miles (40 km) to the west of her better-known sibling, Uluru (*see pp212–15*). In fact the two are conjoined twins. The rock formations are the two tips of an immense curving arm of pebble sandstone buried as deep as 4 miles (6 km) into the bedrock. Now covering an area of more than 8 square miles (21 square km), Kata Tjuta would once have been far larger, perhaps ten times the size of Uluru. However, its chunky, conglomerate composition has rendered it more susceptible to 500 million years of erosion. Whereas Uluru turns its face to the world, deflecting the winds, Kata Tjuta turns inward upon itself and its secrets.

These rocks are surrounded by mystery. Aboriginal tribes are thought to have lived here as long as 10,000 years ago; and, like Uluru, this has been an important Dreamtime site ever since. Many Aboriginal legends involve Kata Tjuta, often describing the great snake Wanambi who is supposed to live in a waterhole at the summit of the tallest dome, Mount Olga, during the rainy season. The dark lines etched into the stone on the eastern side of his waterhole home are the hairs of his beard. When it is dry he moves down into the caves and gorges below, his breath forming the wind that moves through the gullies and clefts in the rock.

Certain Aboriginal ceremonies are still carried out here, and much of the mythology and sacred ritual are a secret kept between only senior tribe members and the rocks themselves. Perhaps the only way to gain an insight into the powerful enigma at the heart of these rocks is to come here and listen to the whispering of the wind as the breath of the ancient snake god Wanambi ebbs and flows.

New South Wales, Australia
LAKE MUNGO

Human beings have inhabited the shores of Lake Mungo for an astonishing length of time. In the 1970s the cremated remains of a woman and the skeleton of a man were unearthed. They had been buried according to Aboriginal ritual around 48,000 years ago, and these burial practices are considered by many to be the world's earliest evidence of a coherent body of spiritual beliefs. The area continues to have sacred significance to Aboriginals today.

According to Aboriginal myth, the lake was originally formed by two magical creatures, Bookoomurri (a dinosaur-like creature) and a giant kangaroo. Archaeologists have discovered that this region was indeed once home to the giant Procoptodon, a marsupial-like creature more than twice the size of the largest kangaroo in existence today.

When Lake Mungo was a real lake (it is now a dry basin), fish and wildlife were to be found in great abundance. The region was formerly inhabited by two tribes – the Paarintji in the north and the Paakantji in the south. For more than 20,000 years, the tribes lived peacefully by the lake-shore, until the lakes started to dry out between 12,000 and 10,000 years ago. Scorched away by the sun, a vast expanse of land punctuated by dunes and sandy outcrops is all that remains of the waters of the lake. On the northeastern shore, extraordinary mesa-like sediment formations rise from the sand dunes, formed from wind and rain erosion. They are known as the Great Walls of China, so named by early Chinese labourers.

More than a hundred burial sites have now been documented in the surrounding area, as well as campfires, middens, quarries, tool-making sites and even footprints imprinted in the clay – testaments to the communities of the past who once flourished here. And hidden artefacts are still constantly being discovered, especially after rainfall. Lake Mungo is a living archaeological treasure trove.

Northern Territory, Australia

NOURLANGIE ROCK

In the Dreamtime, the time of creation in Aboriginal mythology, two spirit ancestors named Namondjok and Namarrgon journeyed westward, creating the features of the landscape as they went. Among these features was the great outcrop known as Nourlangie Rock, which rises dramatically from the Arnhem Plateau in the Northern Territory of Australia.

For at least 20,000 years Aboriginal peoples have used Nourlangie's crevices and overhangs to shelter from monsoon rains. The outcrop is also home to some of the most astonishing and haunting examples of sacred Aboriginal art. On the lower part of the Nourlangie cliffs, known as Anbangbang, are painted scenes depicting Dreamtime spirits, including Namondjok and Namarrgon, their families, and a host of other beings engaged in sacred clan rituals.

Namondjok is supposed to live in the heavens, though a lone boulder standing on Burrunggui, the upper part of Nourlangie, is said to be a feather left behind from his headdress. Namarrgon, the Lightning Man, resides in the land itself, and another solitary boulder is said to be one of his eyes. Visitors are advised to respect the site lest he visit a dire sickness upon them. The rock paintings of Namarrgon show a line arching over him, linking his hands, head and ankles. The line represents lightning, as it is Namarrgon who brings the violent electrical thunderstorms that strike the Arnhem Plateau in the wet season. Striking the clouds with the stone axes on his head, feet and elbows, he splits them to create lightning, the noise tolling out as thunder across the plain.

As at other Aboriginal sites, according to custom, only Aboriginal people have the right to know the details that would fully explain the scenes in the Nourlangie paintings. While Nourlangie's dramatic beauty is open for all to view, the rock retains many of its sacred mysteries.

RIGHT: According to Aboriginal mythology, the vast outcrop of Nourlangie Rock, in the background of this photograph, was created by the spirit ancestors Namondjok and Namarrgon.

Northern Territory, Australia

DEVILS MARBLES

Balanced on the arid land of the Australian Outback is a collection of imposing red granite boulders known by local Aboriginal tribes as the Karlu Karlu. Varying in size from 2 to 20 feet across and strewn over a vast area, they are balanced in precarious, gravity-defying configurations.

These boulders were formed in a two-stage natural process more than a billion years ago. In the first stage, hardened and compressed magma in the Earth's crust came to the surface as granite, and pressure caused it to crack into enormous square blocks. In the second stage, these blocks were weathered and eroded over millions of years to form the great spheres of rock visible today. The Karlu Karlu are, therefore, symbolic of the most ancient beginnings of creation.

There are many Aboriginal legends associated with this site, passed on through the generations in the Dreamtime stories. The Kaytetye, for example, famously believe the boulders to be the fossilized eggs of the Rainbow Snake, a great serpent who pushed up to the Earth's surface and then slithered all over the world, creating the rivers, gorges, seas and mountains.

All the land surrounding the Devils Marbles is considered sacred in Aboriginal lore and although many of the associated legends and rituals have been forgotten over time, the site retains great spiritual importance for the local people. It was once the setting for month-long ceremonies which brought together four different tribes: the Warlpiri, Warumungu, Kaytetye and Alyawarra. They would meet for this period only, dancing and singing to the spirits in the hope that they would bless the land, until the signal came that they should go their separate ways again. Today, the Devils Marbles are in the custodianship of a joint partnership of parks service rangers and representatives of the four tribes associated with the site, reflecting this age-old tradition of sharing.

BELOW: Just a few of the granite boulders known as the Karlu Karlu or Devils Marbles which dominate this part of the arid Outback landscape.

gazetteer

Every care has been taken to ensure that this information is accurate. However, visitors should always check up-to-date travel guides before travelling. Unless stated otherwise, where no opening times have been provided, sites are accessible all year round. Average temperatures are for daytime.

THE AMERICAS

BELIZE

THE GREAT BLUE HOLE, *Lighthouse Reef, pp30–31*

Climate: Air temperature is 79–86˚F (26–30˚C) throughout the year. At a depth of 130 feet / 40 metres, the water temperature is approx. 76˚F (24˚C) throughout the year. Best time to visit is during the dry season in April and May.

Getting there: Nearest airport is Philip Goldson International Airport, a short flight from Belize International Airport. You can then get there by boat from Ambergris Caye and Caye Caulker (approx. 3 hours).

Other: Dive operators can arrange overnight dive trips.

BOLIVIA

TIWANAKU, *near La Paz, pp22–3*

Opening times: Daily (9 am–4:30 pm), all year round.

Climate: Average temperature is cool at 53˚F (12˚C). Most rain falls in the summer (November to March); in winter (April to October) the days are cooler but the sky is generally clear.

Getting there: Nearest airport is La Paz's El Alto International Airport (32 miles / 52 km). The site is then accessible by bus (1½ hours). Rental cars are also available but driving can be difficult, as some roads don't have signs.

Other: On 21st June, the festival of Aymara New Year (*Machaj Mara*) takes place at Tiwanaku, attracting as many as 5,000 people. Buses leave from La Paz at approx. 4 am on this day, to arrive in time for sunrise.

BRAZIL

CHRIST THE REDEEMER STATUE, *Rio de Janeiro, p27*

Opening times: Daily (8.30 am–6.30 pm), all year round.

Climate: Hot and humid summers (November to March), with temperatures as high as 104˚F (40˚C). Winters (June to September) are cool, with temperatures as low as 59˚F (15˚C). Best time to visit is June to August.

Getting there: Nearest airport is Rio de Janeiro Galeão Antonio Carlos Jobim International Airport (13 miles / 20 km away from the statue). Site accessible by road or a 20-minute cog railway journey.

Other: Visitors can reach the foot of the statue either by walking up 220 steps or using a system of elevators.

CANADA

BASILICA OF SAINTE-ANNE-DE-BEAUPRÉ, *Quebec, p26*

Opening times: Daily (8 am–10 pm), all year round.

Climate: Cool to warm summers (June to September) with temperatures in the range 50–77˚F (10–25˚C), and below 0˚F in the winter (November to April). Best time to visit is May to October.

Getting there: Nearest airport is Quebec City International Airport (approx. 20 miles / 32 km away).

Other: The two most popular pilgrimages to the church take place on 26th July (feast of St Anne) and 8th September (feast of the Nativity of Mary).

GUATEMALA

LAKE ATITLÁN, *Panajachel, pp14–15*

Climate: Generally pleasant tropical climate with an average temperature of 80˚F (27˚C). Nights are cool throughout the year. Best time to visit is outside the windy season (November to February).

Getting there: Nearest airport is La Aurora International Airport, Guatemala City (approx. 70 miles / 110 km). Frequent buses go from Guatemala City to Panajachel (approx. 3½ hours). To get around the lake, boats and ferries are available.

Other: Take a cruise from Panajachel to Santiago Atitlán for close-up views of the volcanoes.

MEXICO

PYRAMID OF THE MAGICIAN, *Yucatán, p34*

Opening times: Daily (8 am–5 pm), all year round.

Climate: Hot and humid all year. Average temperature is 82˚F (28˚C). Best months to visit are October, November, April and May.

Getting there: Nearest airport is Mérida (approx. 70 miles / 115 km). The site is accessible by car (approx. 1 hour).

Other: The Pyramid is part of the Uxmal archaeological complex, which has other structures such as the Governor's Palace, the Nunnery Quadrangle and the Ballcourt, all worth visiting.

WELL OF SACRIFICE, *Chichén Itza, p35*

Opening times: Daily (8 am–5 pm), all year round.

Climate: Hot and humid all year round, especially between 12 and 4 pm. Average temperature is 93˚F (34˚C).

Getting there: Nearest airports are Cancún (approx. 75 miles / 120 km) or Mérida (approx. 115 miles / 190 km); from these you can take a bus or drive.

Other: The Chichén Itza complex itself is full of other archaeological structures that are worth visiting, including El Castillo pyramid.

PERU

NAZCA LINES, *Nazca Desert, p13*

Climate: One of the driest places on Earth. Average temperature is 77˚F (25˚C) with temperatures as high as 104˚F (40˚C). Best not to visit during summer (December to March), when the heat can be extreme.

Getting there: Nearest airport is Jorge Chávez International Airport (approx. 10 miles / 16 km northwest of Lima). Buses and rental cars are available between Lima and Nazca (approx. 275 miles / 440 km, 7 hours).

Other: Most visitors hire local planes to view the Lines from the air.

USA

BIGHORN MEDICINE WHEEL, *Wyoming, p12*
Opening times: Daily, mid-June to September, weather permitting.
Climate: On average 12˚F (-11˚C) during winter, with frequent snowfall, and 59˚F (15˚C) during summer. Best to visit May to October.
Getting there: Nearest airports are South Big Horn County Airport (approx. 65 miles / 100 km) and North Big Horn County Airport (approx. 45 miles / 70 km). The site is accessible by car but is a 1.5-mile / 2.4-km walk from the parking area. People with disabilities can use a motorized vehicle to access the site.
Other: Visitors are asked to walk around the wheel in a clockwise direction to honour Native American tradition.

BIG SUR, *California, pp18-21*
Climate: Generally mild, with dry, sunny summers averaging 60˚F (16˚C) and cool, wet winters averaging 54˚F (12˚C). Mid-summer is the most popular time to visit, as there is scarcely any rain. However, the coast can get foggy, particularly in the mornings. April to June is the best time to see the local flora and fauna, while in September and October you can see the fall colours.
Getting there: Nearest airport is Monterey (approx. 30 miles / 48 km) but San Jose (approx. 120 miles / 195 km) has more frequent flights.
Other: Visitors can camp almost anywhere in Big Sur. Make sure you pack both warm- and cold-weather clothing, whatever the time of year, as temperatures can be unpredictable.

BRYCE CANYON, *Utah, pp10-11*
Opening times (visitor centre): Daily, 8 am-4:30 pm

(April); 8 am-8 pm (May to September); 8 am-6 pm (October); 8 am-4 pm (November to March); closed on Christmas and Thanksgiving days.
Climate: Owing to Bryce Canyon's high elevation, temperatures are lower than in other Utah parks, and hiking is comfortable even in summer. Temperatures can reach 83˚F (28˚C) in summer, and drop to 9˚F (-13˚C) in winter.
Getting there: Nearest airport is Cedar City (approx. 80 miles / 130 km); however there are more flights to Las Vegas, Nevada and Salt Lake City airports (all approx. 250–300 miles / 400–480 km). It is best to hire a car as no public transport directly to the park is available.
Other: From May to October you can find more than 170 species of birds nesting around Thor's Hammer.

CANYON DE CHELLY, *Arizona, pp16-17*
Opening times: Daily (8 am-5 pm), all year round except for Christmas Day.
Climate: Temperatures during summer can be as high as 100˚F (38˚C), and in the winter as low as 20˚F (-7˚C). Temperatures can often change significantly over the course of a day.
Getting there: Nearest airports are in Phoenix (approx. 400 miles / 640 km) and Albuquerque (approx. 230 miles / 370 km) from where you can rent a car. There are also trains and buses from Gallup, New Mexico and Flagstaff, Arizona.
Other: Only one trail (the White House trail) can be visited without a Navajo guide.

DEVILS TOWER, *Wyoming, pp28-9*
Opening times: Daily, all year round, except November to May when the visitor centre and camping area are closed. There is a voluntary climbing ban in June when Native Americans conduct sacred ceremonies around the tower.
Climate: Summers have an average max. temperature of 80˚F (27˚C) with some thunderstorms. In winter the average min. temperature is 8˚F (-13˚C).

Getting there: Nearest airports are Gillette (approx. 45 miles / 75 km) and Rapid City (approx. 90 miles / 145 km). The site is most easily accessible by car.
Other: You can climb the famous Durrance Route in 4-6 hours and then rappel down in 1-2 hours.

MAUNA KEA VOLCANO, *Hawaii, pp32-3*
Climate: Cool and damp, even in summer. The mean temperature at Mauna Kea's summit is 32˚F (0˚C) throughout the year, day and night. Winds of up to 50-70 mph / 80-100 kph can blow at the top. Avoid January and February, when winter storms can drop up to 2 feet / 0.6 metres of snow.
Getting there: Nearest airport is Kona International Airport (approx. 70 miles / 115 km from the Onizuka Visitor Center). You will need to join a tour or hire a four-wheel drive as the road is narrow and steep.
Other: Most people visit the volcano at sunset.

PIPESTONE, *Minnesota, pp38-9*
Opening times: Daily, all year round except Thanksgiving, Christmas and New Year's days.
Climate: Generally warm in the summer with temperatures ranging from 60˚F (16˚C) to 80˚F (27˚C). Winter has very low temperatures, sometimes below 0˚F (-18˚C) and parts of the trail become inaccessible due to snow and ice. Best time to visit is May to September.
Getting there: Nearest airport is Sioux Falls Regional Airport (approx. 50 miles / 80 km), from where you can rent a car.
Other: It is unlawful to remove any pipestone without permission. Only Native Americans enrolled in tribes can quarry the stone.

SERPENT MOUND, *Ohio, pp24-5*
Opening times: Daily, all year round, in daylight hours. The museum is open March to October, Saturdays and Sundays, 10 am-5 pm; November to December, Saturdays and Sundays, 10 am-4 pm.
Climate: Warm, pleasant summers with an average temperature of 70˚F (21˚C) and cold winters with an average temperature of 23˚F (-5˚C).

Getting there: Nearest airport is Port Columbus International Airport (approx. 100 miles / 170 km), from where you can rent a car.

Other: The site has an observation tower from where you can get an overview of the serpent effigy.

WRANGELL-ST ELIAS NATIONAL PARK, *Alaska, pp36-7*

Opening times (visitor centre): October to May, Monday to Friday, 8 am–4:30 pm; from Memorial Day to 12th September, daily, 9 am–7 pm; 13th to 30th September, daily, 8 am–4:30 pm.

Climate: Short, warm summers (June and July are the hottest months with high temperatures of over 80˚F / 27˚C) and long, very cold winters with temperatures as low as -40˚F (-40˚C). Best to visit early June to mid-September.

Getting there: Nearest international airport is Anchorage (approx. 250 miles / 385 km), from where the park is a day's drive away. Alternatively, numerous airstrips throughout the park can be reached by private airplane or licensed air taxis from Juneau and Anchorage airports.

Other: On dark winter nights between 12 and 2 am, it is sometimes possible to see the Northern Lights.

EUROPE
CZECH REPUBLIC
PILGRIMAGE CHURCH OF ST JOHN OF NEPOMUK, *Zelená Hora, p71*

Opening times: Daily (9 am–5 pm), May to September, except Mondays; April to October on Saturdays, Sundays and holidays only (9 am–5 pm).

Climate: Temperate, with mild summers and cold winters. Average temperature of 66˚F (19˚C) in summer and 30˚F (-1˚C) in winter.

Getting there: The nearest airport is Kolin (6 miles / 9 km). From Kolin and Prague, there are trains to the Kutná Hora město (0.6 miles / 1 km), Kutná Hora předměstí (0.6 miles / 1 km) or Kutná Hora-Sedlec (1.2 miles / 2 km). From each of these stations you can take a bus or walk to the church.

Other: You can walk around the cloisters to keep out of the heat in summer, and still get great views of the church exterior.

FINLAND
TURKU CATHEDRAL, *Turku, p89*

Opening times: Daily (9 am–7 pm), all year round, with extended hours in summer (9 am–8 pm).

Climate: Warm summers with temperatures as high as 86˚F (30˚C) and cold winters with temperatures as low as 23˚F (-5˚C) and frequent snowfall.

Getting there: Nearest airports are Turku Airport (6 miles / 9 km) and the Helsinki-Vantaa Airport (approx. 110 miles /175 km). There are good bus and train connections from both airports to the site.

Other: English-language services are held every Sunday afternoon and there is live music in the cathedral on most Tuesday evenings.

FRANCE
CARNAC, *Brittany, p52*

Opening times: Daily, all year round. Access is sometimes restricted, especially in the summer, to reduce erosion to the site.

Climate: Warm summers and mild winters, with average temperatures of 77˚F (25˚C) and 48˚F (9˚C) respectively. July and August are the busiest tourist months. Late spring or early autumn are quieter.

Getting there: Nearest airport is St Brieuc (approx. 65 miles / 110 km). The nearest year-round train station is in Auray (8 miles / 13 km). There are also good bus and ferry links.

Other: It takes at least half a day to a day to see all of the alignments. A good way to explore is by bicycle.

ROCAMADOUR, *Gourdon, pp62-3*

Opening times: Daily (9 am–7 pm), all year round.

Climate: Warm summers and mild winters, with average temperatures of 68˚F (20˚C) and 39˚F (4˚C) respectively.

Getting there: Nearest airports are Bergerac (approx. 60 miles / 100 km) and Toulouse (approx. 80 miles / 130 km), from where trains go to Rocamadour via Brive-la-Gaillarde.

Other: There are usually 3–5 tours of Rocamadour per day. The schedules change frequently, and the times are posted at the entrance to the town.

SAINTE-CHAPELLE, *Paris, pp68-9*

Opening times: Daily (9.30 am–6 pm), March to October; November to February (9 am–5 pm).

Closed Christmas and New Year's days and 1st May.

Climate: Warm summers (highs of 81˚F / 27˚C) and cold winters (lows of 34˚F / 1˚C).

Getting there: Nearest airport is Paris Charles de Gaulle International Airport. You can also take the Eurostar to Paris from London, UK. The chapel is then easily accessible by metro, bus or car from central Paris.

Other: Classical-music concerts are often held in the evenings from mid-March to October.

SÉNANQUE ABBEY, *Provence, pp40-41*

Opening times: Daily, all year round. The abbey buildings are accessible by guided tour.

Climate: Driest weather in France with an annual average of 300 days of sunshine. Temperatures range from highs of 84˚F (29˚C) in summer to lows of 37˚F (3˚C) in winter.

Getting there: Nearest airport is Avignon Airport (2.5 miles / 4 km), from where you can hire a car.

Other: The lavender in the fields surrounding Sénanque is usually in bloom from late June to mid-October.

GERMANY
AACHEN CATHEDRAL, *Aachen, pp56-7*

Opening times: Daily, April to October (7 am–7 pm) and November to March (7 am–6 pm).

Climate: Mild summers with temperatures peaking in the low 70s˚F (low 20s˚C). Winter temperatures can drop below 20˚F (-7˚C) and there is often snowfall.

Getting there: Airports with the best transport links are Dusseldorf (approx. 55 miles / 90 km) and Cologne (approx. 50 miles / 80 km). Aachen is accessible by car and there are good bus and rail services.

Other: You will need to take a guided tour of the cathedral in order to catch a glimpse of Charlemagne's throne.

EXTERNSTEINE, *Teutoburger Wald, pp72-3*

Opening times: Monday to Wednesday (10 am– 12 pm, 3–4 pm) and Thursday to Saturday (10 am–12 pm), all year round.

Climate: Temperatures range from 50–68˚F (10–20˚C) in summer to 32–39˚F (0–4˚C) in winter. Frequent rainfall throughout the year.

Getting there: Nearest major airport is Paderborn, from where there are regular trains to Detmold (approx. 30 miles / 45 km from the airport). The site can then be reached by tourist bus.

Other: The Hermannsdenkmal, a 19th-century monument to German nationalism, is only a few miles away.

GREECE

ROUSANOU MONASTERY, *Metéora, pp80–81*

Opening times: Daily (9 am–1 pm and 3.30 pm–6 pm), all year round. Closed Wednesdays in winter.

Climate: Dry, hot summers and cold winters with heavy snowfall. Temperatures often reach 81˚F (27˚C) in summer and fall below freezing during the winter.

Getting there: Nearest airports are Larisa Airport, Kozani Airport and Ioannina Airport (all approx. 37–50 miles / 60–80 km) but you can also fly to Athens International Airport and catch a train, or bus (both approx. 7 hours), to Kalampaka, the city at the foot of the rock towers. From here you can take a taxi or hire a motorcycle to the monastery.

Other: There are several other clifftop monasteries in Metéora that are worth seeing, including the Holy Trinity, Varlaam and Megalo Meteoro.

ICELAND

GOÐAFOSS WATERFALL, *Mývatn, pp48–9*

Climate: Sunny, dry summers and cool, windy winters with average temperatures of 50˚F (10˚C) and 32˚F (0˚C) respectively.

Getting there: Nearest airport is Akureyri International Airport (approx. 60 miles / 100 km). The falls are located in the river Skjálfandafljót. Buses go to nearby Mývatn from Akureyri, Husavik and Egilsstadir. From here, organized tours of the falls are available.

Other: Lake Ljósavatn, just next to the falls, is also worth visiting.

IRELAND

CROAGH PATRICK, *County Mayo, pp64–7*

Opening times (information centre): Daily, April to May (10 am–6 pm); June to August (10 am–7 pm); September to October (11 am–5 pm). Limited opening hours November to March.

Climate: Unpredictable, frosty weather with sometimes torrential rain. Temperatures range from 50–62˚F (10–17˚C) in summer to 38–47˚F (3–8˚C) in winter. The best months for climbing are April to September.

Getting there: Nearest airport is Knock International Airport, from where the mountain is a 45-minute drive. If travelling from outside Europe use either Shannon or Dublin airports, from where there are bus and train links to nearby Westport.

Other: It takes approx. 2 hours to walk to the summit and about 1½ hours to descend.

ITALY

BASILICA OF SAINT FRANCIS, *Assisi, pp96–7*

Opening times: Lower Church open daily, 6 am–7 pm. Upper Church open daily, 8:30 am–7 pm and until 6 pm in winter.

Climate: Hot, dry summers and cold winters. Temperatures range from 64–82˚F (18–28˚C) in summer to 34–45˚F (1–7˚C) in winter.

Getting there: Nearest airport is Perugia, but most international flights go through Roma Fiumicino Airport. You can take a bus from Perugia to Assisi (1 hour), and a bus or a train from Rome to Assisi (up to 2 hours).

Other: Tourist visits during Mass on Sunday mornings are considered inappropriate.

CATHEDRAL OF SANTA MARIA ASSUNTA, *Torcello, Venice, pp44–7*

Opening times: From Easter to Saint Gratus (7th September), Monday to Saturday (6:30 am–8 pm) and Sundays and holidays (7 am–8 pm); 8th September to Easter, Monday to Saturday (6:30 am–12 pm and 3–7 pm) and Sundays and holidays (7 am–12 pm and 3–7 pm).

Climate: Hot, humid summers especially in July and August with average temperatures of 62–80˚F (17–27˚C). Winter has average temperatures of 42–50˚F (6–10˚C) but they can drop to 27˚F (-3˚C).

Getting there: Nearest airport is Marco Polo Airport, Venice. You can also get to Venice by train from most other Italian cities. Torcello can then be reached by water-bus from the Fondamenta Nuove or San Marco, both on the main island of Venice.

Other: From March to October you can climb the cathedral's bell tower for views of the lagoon.

MONTALCINO & THE ABBEY OF SANT'ANTIMO,
Tuscany, pp100–103

Opening times (abbey): Monday to Saturday (10:15 am–12:30 pm, 3–6:30 pm); Sundays and holidays (9:15–10:45 am and 3–6 pm). Visits are not permitted during religious services.

Climate: Hot, breezy summers (highs of 100˚F / 38˚C), and cool winters (lows of 21˚F / -6˚C), with some snowfall. Best time to visit is in spring and summer.

Getting there: Nearest airports are in Pisa (approx. 95 miles / 150 km) and Florence (approx. 70 miles / 110 km). Good rail links from both airports to Chiusi, the nearest station to Montalcino. Roads are generally good in Tuscany and one of the best ways to travel is by car.

Other: Montalcino is famous for its Brunello di Montalcino wine, which you can sample at any of the restaurants and bars in the town or at the surrounding vineyards.

NETHERLANDS

OUDE KERK, *Amsterdam, pp50–51*

Opening times: Monday to Saturday (11 am–5 pm), Sunday (1–5 pm). Closed 30th April (Queen's Day), Christmas and New Year's Days.

Climate: Warm, humid summers (51–77˚F / 11–25˚C) and cold, unpredictable winters (34–44˚F / 1–7˚C).

Getting there: Nearest airport is Amsterdam Airport Schiphol. You can also take the Eurostar to Amsterdam from London, UK via Brussels. The site is then accessible by rail and tram.

Other: For good views of Old Amsterdam, climb the church tower as part of the hourly guided tour.

NORWAY

ALTA FJORD ROCK CARVINGS, *Finnmark, p43*

Opening times: October to April, Monday to Friday (8 am–3 pm), and Saturdays and Sundays (11 am–4 pm); May, daily (8 am–5 pm); June to August, daily (8 am–8 pm); and September, daily (8 am–5 pm). Closed 1st January, 9th to 12th April, 1st May, 17th May, 24th to 26th December and 31st December.

Climate: Summers are cool (50–57˚F / 10–14˚C) and winters below freezing (19–28˚F / -7 to -2˚C).

Getting there: Nearest airport is Alta

(5 miles / 8 km). There are frequent buses to the site from Alta, or you can hire a car.
Other: There are 45 different petroglyph sites at Alta and you can reach most of them via a wooden boardwalk.

AURORA BOREALIS, *pp78-9*
Times to see: September and October, and March and April are when the lights are most likely to appear. They are best viewed during the early evening and at night when it's not overcast.
Where: Various locations in the north of the Northern Hemisphere, such as Norway, Greenland, Iceland, Canada, Alaska and Russia. Some of the best viewing locations are the coasts of the Norwegian counties of Tromso and Finnmark, especially the North Cape (Nordkapp).
Getting there: Airports throughout North Norway such as Tromsø, Kirkenes and Alta. By rail, travel north on the Northern Railway between Trondheim and Bodø. Ferries, boats and buses are also available.

PORTUGAL
ALCOBAÇA MONASTERY, *Alcobaça, pp98-9*
Opening times: Daily, April to September (9 am–7 pm) and October to March (9 am–5 pm).
Climate: Warm summers with temperatures in the late-60s°F (early 20s°C) and mild temperatures in winter rarely dropping below 50°F (10°C).
Getting there: Nearest airport is Lisbon International Airport. Buses run from Lisbon to Alcobaça and take 2 hours. Alternatively you can take a train from Lisbon to Valado dos Frades and then take a bus the last 3 miles (5 km) to Alcobaça.
Other: Don't miss the intricately carved tombs of King Pedro I and Inês de Castro in the monastery transept.

CONVENTO DE CRISTO, *Tomar, pp82-3*
Opening times: Daily, June to September (9 am–6 pm), October to May (9 am–12:30 pm and 2–5 pm).
Climate: Warm summers with temperatures in the late-60s°F (early 20s°C) and mild temperatures in winter rarely dropping below 50°F (10°C).
Getting there: Nearest airport is Lisbon Portela International Airport (approx. 75 miles / 120 km).

There are daily trains from Lisbon to Tomar, and the site is accessible by car.
Other: Look out for the opulent decoration on the church portal, the rotunda (*charola*) and the west window of the chapter house.

SPAIN
TALATÍ DE DALT, *Menorca, pp60-61*
Climate: Warm summers from low to high 70s°F (20s°C) and above, and mild, moderately wet winters with an average temperature of 50°F (10°C). Spring is the best time to visit as it's quieter but the weather is still good.
Getting there: Nearest airport is in Menorca (2.5 miles / 4 km), from where you can take a bus to nearby Mahón (Maó), or hire a car. Alternatively, get a ferry to Mahón from Alcudia or Palma de Mallorca.
Other: A few miles away is Monte El Toro, the highest point on the island. The hill has excellent views and is also home to a 16th-century monastery.

SANTIAGO DE COMPOSTELA, *Galicia, pp74-7*
Opening times: Daily (7 am–9 pm), all year round.
Climate: Warm summers and mild winters with temperatures of 64–8°F (18–20 °C) and 46–50°F (8–10°C) respectively.
Getting there: Nearest airport is Lavacolla Airport (7 miles / 11 km). From here you can take a bus or train to Santiago, or hire a car. You can also take an overnight train or bus to Santiago from Madrid.
Other: The traditional pilgrimage to Santiago de Compostela, the "Way of St James", can take weeks of walking. The two most popular routes are the *Camino Francés* ("French Way"), starting from the French side of the Pyrenees or from Jaca or Roncesvalles on the Spanish side, and the *Camino Portugues* ("Portuguese Way"), starting from Porto in Portugal.

RUSSIA
VALAAM MONASTERY, *Valaam, p70*
Opening times: Variable. Visitors are asked to contact the Pilgrimage Department in St Petersburg (tel. 812 186 99 23; fax 812 252 77 00) or at Valaam (tel. 814 303 82 33) to make an appointment before setting off for the island.

Climate: Valaam has a microclimate which makes its temperature warmer than that of the surrounding areas. Average summer (June to September) temperature is 63°F (17°C) and winter (November to March) temperatures can reach as low as 18°F (-8°C).
Getting there: Nearest airport is Petrozavodsk, from where you can transfer to the Karelian towns of Sortavala, Lahdenpohja, Pitkyaranta and take a boat to Valaam. Alternatively you can catch a cruise boat from St Petersburg or Moscow. Boats from the mainland only run May to October.
Other: There are ten other hermitages that you can visit, some inhabited, others deserted, on Valaam and the nearby islands.

SWEDEN
GAMLA UPPSALA, *Uppsala, p88*
Opening times (church): daily, April to September daily (9 am–6 pm); October to March (9 am–4 pm).
(Museum): May to August, daily (11 am–5 pm); September to April, Wednesdays, Saturdays and Sundays (12–3 pm). Burial mounds can be seen all year round.
Climate: Cool summers (highs of 70°F / 16°C) and cold winters (lows of 23°F / -5°C). Best time to visit is May to September.
Getting there: Nearest airport is Stockholm, from where there are good bus and rail links to Uppsala (approx. 40 minutes). You can then walk or cycle to the church, or take the bus that stops at Vaksalagatan.
Other: The Old Uppsala Museum has exhibitions about the myths and ancient rites associated with the site.

SWITZERLAND
SOGN BENEDETG NEW CHAPEL, *Sumvitg, pp90-91*
Opening times: Monday to Saturday, all year round.
Climate: Mild summers (highs of 64°F / 18°C) and cold winters (lows of 30°F / -1°C).
Getting there: Nearest airport is Zurich International Airport. From here trains go to Sumvitg, changing at Chur (approx. 2½–3 hours). The chapel is 0.6 miles / 1 km from Sumvitg, up a steep road.
Other: Another impressive building designed by

architect Peter Zumthor is within 2 hours driving distance of Sumvitg: Therme Vals, a spa-complex built over a thermal spring in Vals.

UK

KING'S COLLEGE CHAPEL, *Cambridge, England, pp58-9*

Opening times: 6th October to 4th December, 12th January to 12th March and 20th April to 11th June, Monday to Friday (9:30 am–3:30 pm), Saturday (9:30 am–3:15 pm), Sunday (1:15–2:15 pm). Rest of the year (out of term time), Monday to Saturday (9:30 am–4:30 pm), Sunday (10 am–5 pm).
Climate: Warm summers (average of 69˚F / 21˚C) and rainy, windy winters (average of 34˚F / 1˚C). Weather in spring and autumn can be unpredictable.
Getting there: Cambridge is within easy reach of all London airports. Frequent trains run from London's Kings Cross (approx. 45 minutes). Buses from Cambridge station stop near the college. Bicycles are available to hire.
Other: To hear the famous chapel choir, try to catch Evensong, held in term time at 5:30 pm Monday to Wednesday, Fridays and Saturdays, and 3:30 pm on Sundays.

MORVERN, *near Kinloch, Scotland, pp84-7*
Climate: Overall, cool and wet climate with abundant rainfall. The average annual temperature is 48˚F (9˚C).
Getting there: Nearest airports are Edinburgh and Glasgow. Reachable in a few hours from both cities by rail and bus links, but travelling by car is the easiest method.
Other: Loch Teacuis in Morvern is excellent for a number of outdoor activities such as walking, climbing and mountain biking.

THE RING OF BRODGAR, *Orkney, Scotland, p53*
Climate: Breezy, cool summers (average of 54˚F / 12˚C) and windy, cold winters (average of 39˚F / 4˚C). Best to visit April to October.
Getting there: Nearest airport is Kirkwall (16 miles / 26 km). You can also travel to Thurso by train from Inverness, and take a bus that connects to the Orkney ferry at Scrabster, or alternatively travel to Aberdeen by train and take a ferry from there.

Other: Most visitors go to Brodgar at sunset, so arrive earlier in the day if you want to avoid the crowds.

ST PETER-ON-THE-WALL, *Essex, England, pp54-5*
Climate: Warm summers (average of 69˚F / 21˚C) and rainy, windy winters (average of 34˚F / 1˚C). Weather in spring and autumn can be unpredictable.
Getting there: Essex is easy to access from all London airports. Nearest railway station is Southminster (7 miles / 11 km), from where the chapel can be reached by car. The walk from the car park to the chapel takes about 15–20 minutes.
Other: The Bradwell Pilgrimage takes place on the first Saturday in July every year. On this day hundreds of pilgrims walk from St Thomas's Church in Bradwell to St Peter-on-the-Wall for an open-air service and picnic.

THE WHITE HORSE, *Uffington, England, p42*
Climate: Warm summers (average of 69˚F / 21˚C) and wet, sometimes foggy winters (average of 34˚F / 1˚C). Best to visit during summer as it can get very windy on top of the White Horse Hill in winter.
Getting there: Nearest airports are Bristol (approx. 65 miles / 100 km) and London Heathrow (approx. 70 miles / 110 km). The nearest railway station is Swindon and there are good rail links from both airports. The site is accessible by car, bicycle and bus. Buses depart from Faringdon, Wantage and Swindon and stop approx. 600 feet (200 metres) away.
Other: Aside from hiring a plane, the best views are from about 1 mile / 2.4 km to the north of the site, as well as from Dragon Hill, immediately below it.

WISTMAN'S WOOD, *Devon, England, pp92-5*
Climate: Temperate but unpredictable weather, even in summer. Average temperatures range from 69˚F (21˚C) in summer to 34˚F (1˚C) in winter.
Getting there: Nearest airport is Exeter (approx. 35 miles / 56 km). The nearest train station is Newton Abbot (16 miles / 25 km). Although there are local bus services around the Dartmoor National Park, they are somewhat infrequent and the wood is therefore best approached by car. The car park at the Two Bridges Hotel near Princetown is a

25-minute walk from the woods.
Other: If you want to see moorland birds, the best time to visit is mid-April to August.

AFRICA & THE MIDDLE EAST
ARMENIA

KHOR VIRAP MONASTERY, *Ararat Marz, pp132-3*
Opening times: Open daily, all year round.
Climate: Variable weather with very hot summers, June to mid-September (86–95˚F / 30–35˚C) and below freezing temperatures in winter, November to April (can reach as low as -22˚F / -30˚C). Best time to visit is between April and October.
Getting there: Nearest airport is Yerevan Airport (approx. 19 miles / 30 km). There are daily *marshrutka*s (shared minibuses) and buses from Yerevan to Khor Virap that take about 45 minutes. Alternatively you can hire a car at the airport.
Other: If you want to climb down into the famous pit underneath St Gevorg's Chapel, make sure you wear robust shoes.

BOTSWANA

MAKADIKADI SALT PANS, *Makadikadi, pp140-43*
Climate: Dry season is end of April to early November (average of 77˚F / 25˚C); wet season is November to March (average of 86˚F / 30˚C). Best to visit during the dry season.
Getting there: Nearest airport is Maun International Airport (approx. 120 miles / 195 km), from where you can hire a four-wheel drive car.
Other: Most lodges are closed during the wet season and vehicles can get jammed in the mud. However, you can still experience the Salt Pans at this time by going on a fly-in safari.

EGYPT

MOUNT SINAI, *Sinai Peninsula, pp108-9*
Climate: Hot, dry weather for most of the year. Average temperatures during the day are 77–86˚F (25–30˚C) and 50–54˚F (10–12˚C) at night.
Getting there: Nearest airport is Sharm el Shaykh (approx. 55 miles / 90 km). Mount Sinai can only be accessed by road. It is about a 3-hour trip from Sharm el Shaykh to the foot of the mountain.
Other: Time your arrival for approx. 1 am and then climb the mountain in time to watch the sunrise from the summit.

ETHIOPIA

LALIBELA, *Semien Wollo Zone, pp116–19*

Opening times: Daily (8 am–12 pm; 2–5 pm), all year round, but opening hours can be unreliable.

Climate: Dry season is October to May; wet season is June to September. Average temperature remains reasonably consistent at 77˚F (25˚C). Best to visit October to March.

Getting there: Nearest airport is in Lalibela. There are also daily buses from Addis Ababa (approx. 400 miles / 640 km). You can also rent a car with a local driver from Addis Ababa.

Other: Bring a torch so that you can see the interiors of the rock-hewn churches.

IRAN

SHEIKH LOTFOLLAH MOSQUE, *Isfahan, p145*

Opening times: Monday to Thursday and Saturday to Sunday (9 am–9 pm), but opening hours can be unreliable.

Climate: Extremely hot summers (June to August) with temperatures of more than 100˚F (38˚C); generally mild winters (December to February) with temperatures occasionally falling below freezing. Best to visit September to November or March to May when the average temperature is 70˚F (21˚C).

Getting there: Nearest airport is in Isfahan (13 miles / 20 km). The mosque is a short taxi ride from the airport. You can also get to Isfahan by train from Tehran.

Other: Dress conservatively; women must wear a headscarf at all times.

SHRINE OF IMAM REZA, *Mashhad, pp138–9*

Opening times: Daily, all year round.

Climate: Mild summers, June to August (average of 75˚F / 24˚C) and cold winters, December to February (average of 37˚F / 3˚C).

Getting there: Nearest airport is Mashhad International Airport. From Tehran you can also travel to Mashhad by train in 10–14 hours.

Other: Dress conservatively; women must wear a headscarf at all times.

ISRAEL

TEMPLE MOUNT, *Jerusalem, pp120–21*

Opening times: Sunday to Thursday, 7:30–10 am and 12:30–1:30 pm. Closed on religious holidays.

Climate: Hot summers, June to August (88˚F / 31˚C) and mild winters, December to February (41˚F / 5˚C) with some rain. Best to visit in spring or in autumn.

Getting there: Nearest airport is Ben Gurion International Airport (approx. 35 miles / 55 km). Good bus and train connections to Jerusalem from major cities in Israel, and good bus and taxi services in the city. Public transport does not run on *Shabbat* (Saturday), when shared taxis can be used instead.

Other: Keep any non-Muslim religious items such as rosaries and Bibles concealed while on Temple Mount.

JORDAN

PETRA, *Arabah, pp134–7*

Opening times: Daily, approx. 6 am–5 pm (closes at sunset), all year round.

Climate: Overall, hot and dry weather with hardly any rain. Heat is intense between June and September (average of 90˚F / 32˚C). Best to visit mid-January to May when the weather is milder (average of 55˚F / 13˚C).

Getting there: Nearest airport is Queen Alia International Airport (approx. 170 miles / 275 km), just outside Amman. From here you can take a taxi to Amman and then a bus from the Wahdat bus terminal to Arabah.

Other: You can hire a horse and ride into Petra.

MALI

DOGON SHRINES, *Bandiagara, pp126–9*

Climate: Hot desert climate all year round. Average temperatures range from 61˚F (16˚C) to 102˚F (39˚C). Best time to visit is September to November.

Getting there: Nearest airport is Bamako-Sénou International Airport (approx. 400 miles / 640 km). From there you can take a bus or an internal flight to Mopti. Bandiagara can be reached from Mopti by taxi or bus (approx. 2 hours).

Other: You can hire a local Dogon guide and hike to the various villages and their shrines.

THE GREAT MOSQUE, *Djenné, pp104–5*

Opening times: Daily, all year round. Please note that it is forbidden for non-Muslims to enter the actual mosque.

Climate: Hot desert climate with a wet season in July and August. Average annual high temperature over 86˚F (30˚C), average low of 55˚F (13˚C). Best to visit November to February.

Getting there: Nearest airport is Bamako-Sénou International Airport (approx. 250 miles / 400 km). From there you can take a bus or internal flight to Mopti. When the rivers are high, you can take a *pinasse* (traditional boat) from here to Djenné.

Other: The best views of the mosque are from the roofs of the surrounding houses or the nearby Petit Marché.

MOROCCO

BEN YOUSSEF MADRASA, *Marrakesh, p144*

Opening times: Daily, April to September (9 am–7 pm); October to March (9 am–6 pm).

Climate: Dry climate with hot summers, June to August (average of 62–100˚F / 17–38˚C) and cool winters, November to March (average of 39–64˚F / 4–18˚C). Best times for visiting are March to June and September to December.

Getting there: Nearest airport is Marrakesh-Menara Airport (4 miles / 6 km). From here, you can take an Airport Express bus into the city, take a taxi or rent a car. By railway, Marrakesh can be reached from Casablanca, Rabat or Tangier.

Other: The site can get quite busy with large tour groups. Visit at lunchtime or toward the end of the day for a quieter time.

SAUDI ARABIA

MECCA, *Mecca, pp130–31*

Opening times: Forbidden access to non-Muslims. Muslims can visit all year round.

Climate: Dry desert climate with warm winters and hardly any rainfall. Average high temperature is 100˚F (37˚C) in summer (June to August) and minimum 37˚F (3˚C) in winter (December to March). Best to visit during winter when the temperatures are more bearable.

Getting there: Nearest airport is King Abdul Aziz International Airport, or, if travelling by ferry, there is the Jeddah Seaport, both in Jeddah (approx. 45 miles / 70 km). From Jeddah, travel to Mecca by bus, private car or taxi. Note that women are not allowed to drive.

Other: Muslims must first obtain either a *Hajj* or

Umrah (the two different types of pilgrimage) visa before entering Mecca.

SUDAN

MEROË PYRAMIDS, *Meroë, pp122–3*
Climate: Hot and dry summers, June to August (average of 61–88˚F / 16–31˚C), with warm winters, November to March (41–70˚F / 16–28˚C). Best to visit December to February.
Getting there: Nearest airport is Khartoum International Airport (approx. 60 miles / 100 km). Trains go from Khartoum to Shendi, from where the pyramids are only a short taxi-ride away.
Other: You must obtain a special visitor's permit to visit the pyramids from the Antiquities Service in Khartoum.

SYRIA

UMAYYAD MOSQUE, *Damascus, p110*
Opening times: Open daily, all year round, no fixed visiting hours.
Climate: Dry, hot summers, June to August (highs of 100˚F / 38˚C), and cold winters, December to February (lows of 32˚F / 0˚C), sometimes with snowfall. Only moderate temperature variations between day and night.
Getting there: Nearest airport is Damascus International Airport, from where the mosque is a short taxi- or bus-ride away.
Other: Remove your shoes at the door and observe silence during prayers. Dress conservatively; women must wear a headscarf at all times.

TURKEY

HAGIA SOPHIA, *Istanbul, pp114–15*
Opening times: Tuesday to Sunday (9 am–4:30 pm).
Climate: Hot, dry summers, June to September (61–82˚F / 16–28˚C), and mild, rainy winters, November to April (36–52˚F / 2–11˚C). Best time to visit is April to October.
Getting there: Nearest airport is Istanbul Atatürk Airport (12 miles / 20 km). You can also travel to Istanbul by public trains or by the Orient Express (from Hungary, Romania, Greece and Bulgaria). In the city, you can use buses, trams, taxis, the subway or rent a car.
Other: The 17th-century Sultan Ahmed Mosque, or "Blue Mosque" is opposite the Hagia Sophia.

WEST BANK

BETHLEHEM, *Bethlehem Municipality, pp106–7*
Opening times: Church of the Nativity open daily; in summer 6:30 am–12 pm and 2–7.30 pm; in winter 5.30 am–12 pm and 2–5 pm. Grottoes are closed to tourists on Sunday mornings. Rachel's Tomb can be accessed at all times except Sunday to Thursday 10:30 am–1.30 pm, *Shabbat* (Saturday) and holidays.
Climate: Hot, dry summers, June to August (average of 79–86˚F / 26–30˚C), and cool winters, December to February (average of 48–64˚F / 9–18˚C), with some rain. Best to visit in spring or autumn.
Getting there: Nearest airport is Ben Gurion International Airport (approx. 40 miles / 60 km). From Jerusalem take a bus or taxi from Damascus Gate to Bethlehem (approx. 40 minutes).
Other: Be prepared for rigorous questioning at the military checkpoints on the road from Jerusalem.

ZIMBABWE

MATOBO HILLS, *near Bulawayo, pp124–5*
Climate: Dry season is end of April to early November; wet season is November to March. Average temperatures range from 45–84˚F (7–29˚C) during the dry season and 41–70˚F (16–28˚C) during the wet season. Best to visit in April and May or August and September.
Getting there: Nearest airport is Bulawayo Airport (approx. 20 miles / 30 km). During the wet season, four-wheel drive transport is essential.
Other: Organized horseback riding tours are available, and are an unusual way to explore the Matobo National Park.

ASIA

BHUTAN

TAKTSANG MONASTERY, *Paro, pp150–51*
Opening times: Variable hours, contact the Tourism Council of Bhutan before travelling.
Climate: Temperate. Average temperatures range from 15–25˚F (59–77˚C) in summer (June to August) and 3–13˚F (37–55˚C) in winter (late December to mid-February). Best to visit March to May and September to November.
Getting there: Nearest airport is in Paro, from where you can drive to a car park at the foot of the monastery cliff (approx. 20 minutes). You can then

reach the monastery either on foot (2–3 hours) or by a 2-hour mule ride.
Other: No photography is permitted inside the monastery and shoes must be left at the entrance.

CAMBODIA

ANGKOR WAT, *Angkor, pp190–93*
Opening times: Daily, from sunrise to sunset, all year round.
Climate: Tropical climate with hot temperatures ranging from 70–95˚F (21–35˚C) all year round. Best to visit December to April, outside of the monsoon.
Getting there: Nearest airport is in Siem Reap (4 miles / 7 km). You can also get to Siem Reap by bus from Thailand (approx. 6–9 hours), and by bus (5–6 hours) or boat (4–6 hours) from Phnom Penh. You can then hire a car or take a tuk tuk.
Other: To get the best view of the temples in Angkor Wat, consider hiring a private helicopter.

CHINA

MOUNT TAI, *Shandong Province, p196*
Climate: Temperate monsoon climate around the foot of the mountain, highs of 79˚F (26˚C) in summer (May to July) and lows of 23˚F (-5˚C) in winter (November to January). At the top of the mountain it is generally cold throughout the year with sometimes near-freezing temperatures. Best to visit April to November.
Getting there: Nearest airport is Jinan Yaoqiang International Airport (approx. 85 miles / 140 km). From here take the airport shuttle bus or train to Tai'an City. From Tai'an, you can take local buses or hire a taxi to take you directly to the mountain.
Other: It takes about 4 hours to climb up Mount Tai using the most popular east route.

PAGODA FOREST, *Shaolin, p185*
Opening times: Daily (8 am–5:30 pm), all year round.
Climate: Hot, humid summers, June to August (average highs of 84˚F / 29˚C) and generally mild winters, December to March (average lows of 27˚F / -3˚C). There are sometimes typhoons during the wet season (May to October), so best to visit outside of this time.
Getting there: Nearest airport is in Zhengzhou, from where you can take a bus to Shaolin Temple,

changing at Dengfeng (approx. 3 hours). The forest is then a 700-foot / 200-metre walk uphill.

Other: The Shaolin temple complex downhill from the forest is also worth visiting.

TEMPLE OF HEAVEN, *Beijing, p197*

Opening times: Daily, 5 am–9:30 pm in summer, and 6 am–8 pm in winter.

Climate: Hot, rainy summers, June to August (64–88˚F / 18–31˚C), and cold, dry winters, December to March (14–39˚F / -10–4˚C). July and August are the rainiest months. Best to visit in September to October or March to mid-May.

Getting there: Nearest airport is Beijing Capital International Airport (approx. 20 miles / 30 km). Local buses and the subway go near to the Temple of Heaven. You can also take a taxi, hire a bicycle or rent a car with a local driver.

Other: Enter by the south gate (*nan men*) so that you can end your tour with the Hall of Prayer for Good Harvests.

YUNGANG CAVE SHRINES, *Shanxi, pp174-5*

Opening times: Daily (8 am–5 pm), all year round.

Climate: Cold and dry with a lot of rainfall and sometimes sandstorms. Temperatures reach as high as 79˚F (26˚C) in summer (June to August) and fall to below freezing in winter (December to March). Best to visit May to October.

Getting there: Nearest airport is Datong (approx. 10 miles / 16 km from Datong City). The grottoes are a short bus or taxi ride from Datong City.

Other: Photography inside the grottoes is prohibited.

INDIA

BAHÁ'Í LOTUS TEMPLE, *New Delhi, pp180-81*

Opening times: Monday to Saturday (9.30 am–5:30 pm), all year round.

Climate: Extremely hot summers, April to June (average max. 115˚F / 46˚C) and cold winters, November to January (average min. 30˚F / -1˚C). Wet season is late June to mid-September. Best to visit February to April, or September to November.

Getting there: Nearest airport is Indira Gandhi International Airport (14 miles / 23 km). By bus and rail, Delhi can be reached from throughout India, as well as Nepal. You can use public transport to get

to the temple (bus, taxi, subway and rickshaw), or rent a car.

Other: Throughout the day, educational films about the Bahá'í Lotus Temple and the Bahá'í Faith are screened at the temple's Information Centre (around seven short films per day).

THE BODHI TREE, *Bihar, pp172-3*

Opening times: Mahabodhi Temple complex opens daily (5 am–9 pm).

Climate: Extremely hot summers, April to mid-June (average max. 117˚F / 47˚C) and cold winters, December and January (average min. 38˚F / 4˚C). Wet season is June to September. Best to visit October and November or February and March.

Getting there: Nearest airport is in Patna (approx. 65 miles / 105 km), from where you can take a bus or a train to Gaya, and then it is a short bus or taxi ride to Bodhgaya. Gaya also has good train links to Varanasi, New Delhi, Kolkata and Puri.

Other: The biggest festival in Bodhgaya takes place in May for *Buddha Jayanti* (Buddha's birthday).

DARGAH OF NIZAMUDDIN, *New Delhi, pp176-7*

Opening times: Daily, from sunrise to sunset, all year round.

Climate: Extremely hot summers, April to June (average max. 115˚F / 46˚C) and cold winters, November to January (average min. 30˚F / -1˚C). Wet season is late June to mid-September. Best to visit February to April, or September to November.

Getting there: Nearest airport is Indira Gandhi International Airport (approx. 14 miles / 23 km). By bus and rail, Delhi can be reached from throughout India, as well as Nepal. You can use public transport to get to the mausoleum (bus, taxi, subway and rickshaw) or rent a car.

Other: On Thursday evenings, except during Ramadan, Qawwali (Sufi devotional) musicians perform at the shrine.

ELLORA CAVES, *Maharashtra, pp170-71*

Opening times: Daily, except Tuesdays, 9 am until sunset (around 5.30 pm).

Climate: Three main seasons (summer from March to May, wet season from June to September, and winter season from November to February), ranging from hot to mild temperatures.

Average temperature is 90˚F (32˚C) in summer and 61˚F (16˚C) in winter. Best to visit October to February.

Getting there: Nearest airport is Aurangabad (9 miles / 15 km). Trains run between Mumbai and Aurangabad daily (approx. 7 hours). From Aurangabad you can take a taxi or bus to the caves.

Other: You can hire a guide at the ticket office in front of the Kailasa Temple for up to 4 hours.

GOLDEN TEMPLE, *Amritsar, pp202-5*

Opening times: Daily, in summer 7:30 am–7:30 pm; in winter 8 am–7 pm.

Climate: Summer (April to June) has temperatures as high as 100˚F (43˚C); rainy season (July to September) has average annual rainfall levels of 18–38 inches / 46–96 cm; winter (October to March) has temperatures as low as 40˚F (4˚C). Best time to go is between November and March.

Getting there: Nearest airport is Amritsar Airport, from where you can take a short taxi or bus ride to the temple. There are also frequent buses from Delhi (approx. 10 hours) and Chandigarh (approx. 7 hours), and an express train from Delhi (approx. 7 hours).

Other: Try *langar*, a free sanctified meal prepared daily by worshippers and served at the temple.

JAMA MASJID, *New Delhi, pp146-9*

Opening times: Daily, all year round. Visiting hours for non-Muslims are 8.30 am–12:30 pm and 1:45 pm until 30 minutes before sunset.

Climate: Extremely hot summers, April to June (average max. 115˚F / 46˚C), and cold winters, November to January (average min. 30˚F / -1˚C). Wet season is late June to mid-September. Best to visit February to April, or September to November.

Getting there: Nearest airport is Indira Gandhi International Airport (13 miles / 21 km). By bus and rail, Delhi can be reached from throughout India, as well as Nepal. You can use public transport to get to the mosque (bus, taxi, subway and rickshaw) or rent a car.

Other: Dress conservatively; women must wear a headscarf at all times, and you will need to take off your shoes and wash your feet before entering the mosque. For a small fee you can climb the mosque's southern minaret for excellent views of the city (women must be accompanied by a male).

JANOG & THE TEMPLES OF HIMACHAL PRADESH, *pp194-5*

Opening times: Vary from village to village.

Climate: Temperate summers, mid-April to June (average of 57–68˚F / 14–20˚C), and extremely cold winters, November to March (lows of 20˚F / -7˚C) with some snowfall. Wet season is July to September. Best time to visit is April to June.

Getting there: Nearest airport is Shimla Airport (approx. 25 miles / 40 km). From Delhi you can take a train to Kalka (approx. 5½ hours) and then change trains for Shimla (approx. 5 hours). Most temples are accessible by car. Janog is approx. 1 hour's drive from Shimla.

Other: Himachal Pradesh's main pilgrim destinations are Manikaran, Rawalsar, Paonta Sahib, Shimla, Kullu and Chamba.

RANAKPUR TEMPLE, *Rajasthan, pp156-7*

Opening times: Daily, 12–5 pm for non-Jains.

Climate: Warm and dry throughout the year, except during the monsoon season (June to September). The average maximum and minimum temperatures range from 72 to 108˚F (22 to 42˚C). Best to visit October to March.

Getting there: Nearest airport is in Udaipur (approx. 35 miles / 60 km), from where there are direct buses to the temple (approx. 3 hours). You can also hire rickshaws and taxis, and cars with a local driver.

Other: Visit the other temples in the complex, including the Parsavanath Temple, the Amba Mata Temple and the Surya Temple.

INDONESIA

BOROBUDUR, *Java, pp198-201*

Opening times: Daily, 7 am–6 pm.

Climate: Hot and humid with a dry season (May to September) and a wet season (October to April). Average temperatures range from 66 to 86˚F (19 to 30˚C). The dry season is the best time to visit.

Getting there: Nearest airport is Adisucipto International Airport in Yogyakarta. Yogyakarta can also be reached by trains and buses from within Java, and buses from Bali. Getting from Yogyakarta

to Borobudur takes about 40 minutes by car. You can rent cars with a driver from the airport or from hotels, or hire scooters or bicycles.

Other: The Hindu temples of Prambanan (20 minutes from Yogyakarta) are also worth visiting.

JAPAN

FUSHIMI INARI SHRINE, *Kyoto, pp206-7*

Opening times: Daily, from sunrise to sunset, all year round.

Climate: Warm overall, with hot and humid summers. Temperatures range from 64 to 91˚F (18 to 33˚C) in summer (June to August) and 30 to 63˚F (-1 to 17˚C) in winter (mid-November to early March). Wet season is in June. Best time to visit March to April or September to November.

Getting there: Nearest airport is Kansai International Airport in Kyoto (approx. 70 miles / 115 km). From here you can take a train to Fushimi-Inari Station (approx. 2 hours).

Other: It takes approx. 2 hours to walk along the shrine's whole trail.

MIYAJIMA ISLAND, *Hatsukaichi, pp166-9*

Climate: Hot, humid summers, June to August (64–87˚F / 18–31˚C), and generally mild, sunny winters, December to February (32–52˚F / 0–11˚C). Wet season is mid-June to mid-July. Best time to visit is end of March, April, May and early June.

Getting there: Nearest international airport is Kansai International Airport in Kyoto (approx. 270 miles / 430 km). From here you can take a train to Hiroshima (approx. 2 hours) and then on to the Miyajima-guchi Station (approx. 45 minutes). From here you can board a ferry to Miyajima Island (approx. 30 minutes).

Other: As well as visiting the shrine, walk around the island's nature trails such as the Uguisu Walk, the Momiji Walk, the Asebi Walk and the Tsutsumigaura Nature Walk.

RYOANJI ZEN DRY GARDEN, *Kyoto, pp158-61*

Opening times: Daily, March to November, 8 am–5 pm; December to February, 8:30 am–4:30 pm.

Climate: Warm overall, with hot and humid summers. Temperatures range from 64 to 91˚F (18 to 33˚C) in summer (June to August) and 30 to 63˚F (-1 to 17˚C) in winter (mid-November to early

March). Wet season is in June. Best time to visit March to April or September to November.

Getting there: Nearest airport is Kansai International Airport (approx. 75 miles / 120 km). Reach the Zen Dry Garden either by taking a 2.5-hour train ride to Ryoanji-Michi Station or by bus.

Other: Visit in the morning when the garden is at its most tranquil.

MYANMAR

SHWEDAGON PAGODA, *Rangoon, p164*

Opening times: Daily (4 am–10 pm), all year round.

Climate: Hot all year round with average temperatures of 86–95˚F (30–35˚C). Best to visit just after the wet season (June to October).

Getting there: Nearest airport is Yangon (Rangoon) Airport (10 miles / 16 km). By rail and bus, Rangoon can be reached from Mandalay in approx. 15 hours. To get around Rangoon, it's best to use taxis as buses can be overcrowded and chaotic. Note that car rental is not permitted to foreigners.

Other: Dress conservatively when visiting the site, with knees and elbows covered at all times.

SOUTH KOREA

CHEJU ISLAND, *p184*

Climate: Hot, wet summers, June to August (max. 92˚F / 33˚C), and cold, dry winters, December to February (min. 34˚F / 1˚C). Toward end of summer, there may be typhoons.

Getting there: Nearest airport is Jeju International Airport. You can also fly to Busan and Incheon airports in mainland South Korea and then take an overnight ferry. To move around the island, rent a car or bicycle, or use the local buses and taxis.

Other: Visit the Chejudo Folklore and Natural History Museum, which exhibits volcanic rocks, folk crafts, and flora and fauna from the island.

SRI LANKA

ARANKALE FOREST MONASTERY, *North Western Province, pp182-3*

Climate: Hot and humid, average temperatures range from 72 to 88˚F (22 to 31˚C). Best to visit outside of the two main monsoon seasons (May to July and December to January).

Getting there: Nearest airports are Victoria Resevour Kandy Airport (approx. 25 miles / 40 km)

and Bandaranaike International Airport in Colombo (approx. 60 miles / 95 km). There are frequent buses from both Colombo (approx. 5 hours) and Kandy (approx. 1 hour) to Kurunagala from where Arankale is a taxi ride (16 miles / 25 km).

Other: In the mornings, Arankale Forest is a great place for bird watching.

HOLY FOOTPRINT, *Adam's Peak, pp162-3*

Climate: Warm throughout the year (average annual high temperatures over 86°F / 30°C). Best to visit outside of the two monsoon seasons (May to July and December to January).

Getting there: Nearest airport is Bandaranaike International Airport (approx. 80 miles / 130 km). In the pilgrimage season (December to May), buses run to the town of Dalhousie just below the mountain from Kandy (approx. 1 hour), Nuwara Eliya (approx. 2 hours) and Colombo (approx. 2 hours). Outside of the pilgrimage season, you can take a bus or train to Hatton or Maskeliya before taking a taxi to Dalhousie.

Other: The routes up the mountain are illuminated only during the pilgrimage season. You can still do the walk, however – just make sure that you bring a torch.

THAILAND

AYUTTHAYA, *Ayutthaya Province, pp152-5*

Climate: Hot and humid, average temperatures range from 71 to 96°F (22 to 36°C). Best to visit November to February, outside the monsoon season.

Getting there: Nearest airport is in Bangkok (approx. 60 miles / 95 km), from where there are good bus and rail links to Ayutthaya. There are also boat cruises from Bangkok to the Chao Phraya river in Ayutthaya. Ayutthaya can be explored on foot or bicycles. Buses, taxis, trams and tuk tuks are also available.

Other: Dress modestly when visiting the temples.

TIBET

LHASA, *Lhasa Prefecture, pp186-9*

Climate: Cold winters and warm summers. Temperatures can reach highs of 72°F (22°C) in June and lows of 14°F (-10°C) in January. Best time to visit is April to October. Temperature drops

significantly at night, even if the day has been sunny, so always bring warm clothes.

Getting there: Nearest airport is Lhasa Gonggar Airport in Tibet, and there are frequent flights from Chengdu and Kathmandu. There are regular trains to Lhasa from Beijing, via Xining/Lanzhou, Chengdu and Xi'an. From Beijing the train is a 2-night journey. From the station you can take a short bus or taxi ride into town.

Other: Make sure you visit the Jokhang, the Potala and the Barkhor pilgrim circuit.

MOUNT KAILASH, *Gangdisê Mountains, p165*

Climate: Unpredictable mountain climate with warm summers, June to August (highs of 84°F / 29°C) and very cold winters, November to March (lows of 16°F / -9°C).

Getting there: Nearest airport is Lhasa Gonggar Airport in Tibet and the nearest railway station is in Lhasa (*see above*). You can rent a jeep and a driver from Lhasa to take you to the mountain.

Other: Monastery accommodation is sometimes available; however it's advisable to carry your own tents and food with you. Yaks and porters can be hired in Darchen, at the foot of the mountain.

VIETNAM

HA LONG BAY, *Quảng Ninh, pp178-9*

Climate: Two main seasons: hot and rainy summer (May to September) and drier, cool winter (December to March). Average temperatures range from 60 to 77°F (15 to 25°C). Best to visit October to May.

Getting there: Nearest airport is Hanoi International Airport (approx. 100 miles / 170 km). From here you can take a public bus (approx. 6 hours) or a private taxi (approx. 3½ hours). You can also get to Ha Long Bay by boat from Haiphong (approx. 45 miles / 75 km) or Hanoi (approx. 100 miles / 165 km).

Other: Take one of the boat cruises that travel through the bay and stop at the various caves.

AUSTRALASIA & THE PACIFIC

AUSTRALIA

BUNGLE BUNGLE, *The Kimberley, pp210-11*

Opening times: Visitor centre open May to October, daily (8 am–12 pm and 1–4 pm). Camps are closed mid-October to April.

Climate: Average maximum temperatures range from 90 to 100°F (32–100°C) and the nightly minimum rarely falls below 59°F (15°C). Best to visit during the dry season (May to June).

Getting there: Nearest airport is Kununurra (approx. 155 miles / 250 km), from where you can hire a car. To access the last strip of the road leading to the Bungles (approx. 34 miles / 55 km long) you will need a four-wheel drive. Most people view the Bungle Bungles by air (by plane or helicopter).

Other: Climbing the rock towers in the Bungle Bungles is strictly prohibited due to their fragile nature.

CARNARVON GORGE, *Queensland, p217*

Opening times (visitor centre): Daily, 8–10 am and 3–5 pm.

Climate: Very hot and humid summers, November to March (highs of 96°F / 36°C), while in winter (June to August) temperatures can drop to 28°F (-2°C).

Getting there: Nearest airports are in Roma (approx. 155 miles / 250 km) and Emerald, (approx. 150 miles / 240 km), from where you can rent a car. If there has been rainfall you will need a four-wheel drive for the gravel road that leads into the park.

Other: Visit the Moss Garden and the Ward's Canyon, both part of the Carnarvon National Park (approx. 2 miles / 4 km and 3 miles / 5 km from the park's picnic area, respectively).

DEVILS MARBLES, *Northern Territory, pp224-5*

Climate: Semi-arid, with hot summers, November to April (73–93°F / 23–34°C), and cool winters, May to October (68–92°F / 20–33°C). In winter, temperatures can drop below freezing at night. Best months to visit are June and July.

Getting there: Nearest airports are in Darwin and Alice Springs, from where you can get a chartered flight to the Tennant Creek Airport (approx. 60 miles / 100 km from Devils Marbles). Alternatively, you can reach Tennant Creek by rail from Alice Springs, or by bus from Darwin or Alice Springs. From Tennant Creek you can rent a car and drive to the site (approx. 1 hour).

Other: Just north of Tennant Creek are the Devils Pebbles. A more compact version of the Devils Marbles, the Pebbles also have great sacred significance to the local people.

KATA TJUTA, *Northern Territory, p220*
Opening times: Park opens at sunrise and closes at sunset all year round. Information Desk open daily, 8 am–5 pm. Cultural Centre open daily, 7 am–6 pm. Park Administration open daily, 8 am–4:30 pm.
Climate: Hot summers, October to April (57–100°F / 14–38°C), with cooler winters, May to September (37–79°F / 3–26°C). In winter, temperatures can drop below freezing at night.
Getting there: Nearest airport is Ayers Rock (Connellan) Airport in Yulara, from where you can get a bus to the Uluru-Kata Tjuta National Park, or rent a car. Alternatively, Alice Springs Airport is approx. 6 hours away by car.
Other: Try either the fairly difficult Valley of the Winds Walk or the easier Walpa Gorge Walk.

LAKE MUNGO, *New South Wales, p221*
Opening times (visitor centre): Monday to Friday, 8:30 am–12 pm and 1–4:30 pm.
Climate: Variable, with extreme temperatures as high as 104°F (40°C) in the summer (especially between January and February), and below 32°F (0°C) in winter. Best to visit March to October.
Getting there: Nearest airport is Pooncarie Airport (approx. 55 miles / 85 km), from where you can drive to Mungo National Park. Note that roads in and around the park can become inaccessible following rainfall.
Other: Mobile phones do not work at the site and there is no food or car fuel available near the park.

NOURLANGIE ROCK, *Northern Territory, pp222-3*
Opening times: Park opens at sunrise, closes at sunset all year round.
Climate: Dry season, April to September (average of 90°F / 32°C); wet season, January to March (average of 91°F / 33°C). The "build up" season between October and December is very humid and hot (average of 100°F / 37°C). Best to visit during the dry season.
Getting there: Nearest airport is Darwin (approx.

160 miles / 255 km). From here you can hire a car, or take a coach service direct to Kakadu National Park.
Other: Visit the Aboriginal rock art sites of Ubirr and Nanguluwur, also in the park.

ULURU, *Northern Territory, pp212-15*
Opening times: Park opens at sunrise, closes at sunset all year round. Information Desk open daily, 8 am–5 pm. Cultural Centre open daily, 7 am–6 pm. Park Administration open daily, 8 am–4:30 pm.
Climate: Hot summers, October to April (57–100°F / 14–38°C), with cooler winters, May to September (37–79°F / 3–26°C). In winter, temperatures can drop below freezing at night.
Getting there: Nearest airport is Ayers Rock (Connellan) Airport in Yulara, from where you can get a bus to the Uluru-Kata Tjuta National Park, or rent a car. Alternatively, Alice Springs Airport is approx. 6 hours away by car.
Other: Camping is not permitted at the Uluru-Kata Tjuta National Park.

FRENCH POLYNESIA

TAPUTAPUATEA, *Raiatea Island, p216*
Climate: Two main seasons – hot and humid from November to March with frequent rainfalls in January and February, and relatively cool and dry from April to October. The average temperature varies only between 75 and 90°F (24 and 32°C) throughout the year.
Getting there: Nearest airport is Raiatea Airport in Uturoa, from where Taputapuatea is 1 hour's drive (it is best to hire a four-wheel drive). The site can also be reached by boat via the Faaroa river.
Other: Visit Raiatea's other attractions such as Mount Temehani and the Faaroa river.

NEW ZEALAND

AORAKI/MOUNT COOK, *South Island, pp208-9*
Opening times (National Park): Daily, January to April, 8:30 am–5 pm; May to December, 8:30 am–4:30 pm.
Climate: In Aoraki/Mount Cook village, there are warm summers, December to February (highs of 90°F / 32°C) and very cold, snowy winters, June to August (lows of 9°F / -13°C). The temperature at

the mountain summit is at least 50°F (28°C) lower than that in Aoraki/Mount Cook village, and there are often strong winds.
Getting there: Nearest international airports are in Christchurch and Queenstown. From here you can take a charter flight to the one of the four Mackenzie-based airports at Glentanner, Mount Cook, Lake Pukaki and Lake Tekapo, from where you can drive to Aoraki/Mount Cook village in under an hour. Alternatively, you can take a bus from Christchurch, Queenstown or other major centres to Twizel or Lake Tekapo and drive on from there – this journey can take a full day.
Other: If you intend to climb the mountain, a permit won't be necessary but you will be requested to complete a trip intentions form at the Department of Conservation visitor centre.

MOUNT RUAPEHU, *Tongariro National Park, pp218-19*
Opening times (visitor centre): Daily, November to March, 8 am–6 pm; April to October, 8 am–5 pm.
Climate: Variable temperatures throughout the year. In summer (December to March) temperatures reach 77°F (25°C), dropping to 14°F (-10°C) in winter (June to August).
Getting there: Nearest airport is Auckland International Airport (approx. 220 miles / 350 km from Turangi, the nearest town to Tongariro National Park). The park is then a short car or bus ride away.
Other: In the summer you can take a guided hike to the edge of the crater lake at the summit of Mount Ruapehu.

index

picture credits

The publisher would like to thank the following people, museums and photographic libraries for permission to reproduce their material. Every care has been taken to trace copyright holders. However, if we have omitted anyone we apologize and will, if informed, make corrections to any future edition.

t = top   b = bottom

Pages 2–3 AWL images/Antonia Tozer; 5 SuperStock/Robert Harding; 10–11 AWL images/Alan Copson; 12 Getty Images/Courtney Milne; 13 © Stéphane Compoint; 14–15 AWL images/Michele Falzone; 16 Getty Images/Stone/Andy Glass; 17 Corbis/Jose Fuste Raga; 18t Photolibrary.com/Animals Animals/Rich Reid; 18b Photolibrary.com/Radius Images; 20 Photolibrary.com/White/Don Smith; 21 Photolibrary.com/Pixtal Images; 22 Axiom/Andy Kerry; 23 Axiom/Guy Marks; 24–5 Superstock/Tony Linck; 26 Photolibrary.com/Jupiterimages; 27 Axiom/Chris Coe; 29 Photolibrary.com/Animals Animals/Gordon & Cathy Illg; 30 4 Corners/SIME/Simeone Giovanni; 31 SuperStock/Karen G. Schulman; 32–3 Getty Images/Sami Sarkis; 34 Superstock/Hemis.fr; 35 SuperStock/age fotostock/Matz Sjoberg; 36–7 SuperStock/age fotostock/Alan Majchrowicz; 39 Photographers Direct/Cathy Jones; 40–41 Corbis/Herbert Kehrer; 42 Alamy/David Newham; 43 Photolibrary.com/imagebroker.net/Gerhard Zwerger-Schoner; 44 4 Corners/SIME/Fantuz Olimpio; 45 Photolibrary.com/Tips Italia/Guido Alberto Rossi; 46 Scala; 47 Scala; 48–9 AWL images/Michele Falzone; 50–51 AKG-images/Bildarchiv Monheim; 52 Axiom/Hemis; 53 David Lyons; 54 Flickr/Coldmountain/Nick Watts; 55 David Laws; 56 AKG-images/Bildarchiv Monheim; 57 AKG-images/Erich Lessing; 58–9 Alamy/Terence Waeland; 60t Antonio Cerezuela, Seville; 60b Antonio Cerezuela, Seville; 62–3 AWL images/Doug Pearson; 65t Lonely Planet/Gareth McCormack; 65b 4 Corners/SIME/Rellini Maurizio; 66–67 Photolibrary.com/The Irish Image Collection; 68 AKG-images/Joseph Martin; 69 Sonia Halliday Photographs; 70 Alamy/RIA Novosti; 71 Alamy/isifa Image Service s.r.o./Jiri Berger; 72–3 Alamy/vario images/McPhoto; 74 Photolibrary.com/Robert Harding/R H Productions; 75 Photolibrary.com/Hemis/Hervé Hughes ; 76 AKG-images/Andrea Jemolo; 77 Photolibrary.com/F1 Online/Felix Stenson; 78–9 Photographers Direct/John Jordan, Helsinki; 80–81 AWL images/Peter Adams; 82–3 AWL images/Michele Falzone; 84 Alamy/Richard Childs Photography; 86–7 Alamy/Graham Uney; 88 Alamy/Nordicphotos/Anders Tukler; 89 Alamy/Antje Schulte; 90 Mark McCormick; 91 Photographers Direct/Emy Smith; 92–3 Photoshot/Woodfall; 94 Photolibrary.com/Britain on View/Nature Picture Library; 95 Photolibrary.com/Britain on View/Adam Burton; 96–7 4 Corners/SIME/Spila Riccardo; 98 Art Archive/Chester Brummel; 99 Getty Images/Michele Falzone; 100 4 Corners/SIME/Fantuz Olimpio; 101 SuperStock/age fotostock/Bruno Morandi; 102–3 4 Corners/SIME/Da Ros Luca; 104 Axiom/Chris Caldicott; 105 AWL images/Nigel Pavitt; 106 fotoLibra/Yossi ROR/Ulrich W. Sahm; 107 Photographers Direct/Patrick Ellis; 108–9 Getty Images/National Geographic/Kenneth Garrett; 110 Corbis/Frédéric Soltan; 111 Alamy/dbimages; 112 Alamy/Images & Stories; 112–13 Angelo Hornak; 114 AWL images/Gavin Hellier; 115 AKG-images/Erich Lessing; 116 Photolibrary.com/Tips Italia/Franco Taddio; 117 Robert Harding/Andrew McConnell; 118 Axiom/Chris Caldicott; 119 Photolibrary.com/JTB Photo; 120 Corbis/Annie Griffiths Belt; 121 AWL images/Jon Arnold; 122–3 AWL images/Nigel Pavitt; 125t Alamy/United Archives GmbH/KPA/Mauthe, Markus; 125b Alamy/Images of Africa Photobank/Friedrich von Horsten; 126 Getty Images/National Geographic/Martin Gray; 127 Photolibrary.com/JTB Photo; 128–9 Photolibrary.com/JTB Photo; 130 Getty Images/Stone/Nabeel Turner; 131 Getty Images/Reza; 132–3 SuperStock/age fotostock/Wojtek Buss; 134 Axiom/Jon Spaull; 135 Axiom/Hemis; 136–7 Axiom/Hemis; 138 Corbis; 139 Corbis/Kazuyoshi

Nomachi; **140t** Getty Images/Gallo Images/Wim Van Den Heever; **140b** AWL images/Nigel Pavitt; **142-3** Axiom/Guy Marks; **144** Axiom/Chris Caldicott; **145** Getty images/Lonely Planet Images/Holger Leue; **146** Corbis/Reuters/Kamal Kishore; **147** Axiom/Karoki Lewis; **148-9** Corbis/epa/Anindito Mukherjee; **150** AWL images/Paul Harris; **151** Axiom/Doug McKinlay; **152** Axiom/Hemis; **153** AWL images/Peter Adams; **154-5** AWL images/Travel Pix Collection; **155** Axiom/Hemis; **156-7** Getty Images/Image Bank/Donata Pizzi; **158t** Photolibrary.com/Claire Takacs; **158b** Photolibrary.com/Claire Takacs; **160-61** Getty Images/Stone/Paul Chesley; **162-3** Robert Harding/David Beatty; **164** Axiom/Chris Caldicott; **165** Axiom/Ian Cumming; **166t** AWL images/Gavin Hellier; **166b** Getty Images/Sebun Photo/Hiroyuki Yamaguchi; **167** Corbis/B.S.P.I.; **168-9** Getty Images/Larry Dale Gordon; **169** AWL images/Christian Kober; **170** Robert Harding/Adam Woolfitt; **171** Photolibrary.com/Tips Italia/Luca Invernizzi Tettoni; **172** Photolibrary.com/Cusp/Bruno Levy; **173** Getty Images/Image Bank/Eric Meola; **174** Axiom/Timothy Allen; **175** Axiom/Timothy Allen; **176t** Alamy/Imagestate/Mark Henley; **176b** Fabian Foo; **178-9** AWL images/Danita Delimont Stock; **180-81** Axiom/Ian Cumming; **182t** Luxshmanan; **183b** Luxshmanan; **184** Photolibrary.com/JTB Photo; **185** Photolibrary.com/Frederic Soreau; **186** Axiom/Ian Cumming; **187t** Axiom/Ian Cumming; **187b** Axiom/Ian Cumming; **188-189** Axiom/Ian Cumming; **190-91** Axiom/Peter Rayner; **192t** AWL images/Walter Bibikow; **192b** AWL images/David Bank; **193** Axiom/Marc Jackson; **194** Corbis/Paul C. Pet; **195** Shabbir Khambaty and Swapnil Bhole; **196** Getty Images/Keren Su; **197** AWL images/Christian Kober; **198-9** Alamy/Mireille Vautier; **200** Getty Images/Stone+/joSon; **200-201** Getty Images/Image Bank/Philippe Bourseiller; **202** Alamy/Yadid Levy; **203** Corbis/epa/Raminder Pal Singh; **204-5** Robert Harding/Jeremy Bright; **206-7** Getty images/Lonely Planet Images/Frank Carter; **208-9** AWL images/Christian Kober; **210** Photolibrary.com/Ted Mead; **211** Photolibrary.com/Roel Loopers; **212** Photolibrary.com/Imagestate/Martin Ruegner; **213** Photolibrary.com/Ted Mead; **214** Photolibrary.com/E&E Image Library; **214-15** AWL images/Danita Delimont Stock; **216** Corbis/Douglas Peebles; **217** Corbis/Theo Allofs; **218-19** Getty Images/Image Bank/Laurie Noble; **220** AWL images/Danita Delimont Stock; **221** Corbis/Dave G. Houser; **222-3** Photolibrary.com/Radius Images; **224-5** Getty Images/Image Bank/Ted Mead.

ADDITIONAL PICTURE CAPTIONS

FRONT COVER IMAGE: Mount Wuyi in Nanping, southeast China. The remains of more than 60 Taoist temples and monasteries have been discovered on Wuyi's slopes. Mountains are considered sacred in China, and are viewed as columns that connect heaven and Earth. (*See also p196.*)

PAGES 2-3: The silhouettes of some of the latticed stupas on the upper terraces of Borobudur in Indonesia. (*See also pp198-201.*)

PAGE 5: A priest emerges from Bete Amanuel, one of the rock-hewn churches of Lalibela, Ethiopia. (*See also pp116-19.*)

acknowledgments

The publisher would like to thank the following for their invaluable text contributions: Peter Bently, Rachael Withers, Archie Bland, Cordelia Jenkins, Sarah Shuckburgh, Christopher Middleton, Tony Allan and Graham Simmons.